THE BUTLER'S PANTRY™

RECIPES FOR ALL SEASONS

Happy Cooking

(signature)

EILEEN BERGIN grew up with good food, cooking and family
meals as an essential way of life, and was an accomplished home cook
before she started to learn to cook professionally. She has worked in
the food industry for over twenty-five years and is the founder of the
extremely successful catering service and chain of quality food shops,
The Butler's Pantry. Based in Dublin, The Butler's Pantry pioneered
the market in take-home, fresh, wholesome food when it opened its
first tiny store on Mount Merrion Avenue in Blackrock in 1987. She
remains to this day passionate about 'real food' and all its benefits,
is a member of 'Slow Food', and, along with her partner Jacquie
Marsh, is the recipient of numerous awards for her business.

She lives in County Wicklow with her husband and family and, when
she is not cooking, she loves travelling to France and Spain, skiing,
tennis and entertaining family and friends.

THE
BUTLER'S
PANTRY™

RECIPES FOR ALL SEASONS

EILEEN BERGIN

Photographs by Denis Bergin,
assisted by Cathy Treacy

THE O'BRIEN PRESS
DUBLIN

First published 2007 by The O'Brien Press Ltd.
12 Terenure Road East, Rathgar, Dublin 6, Ireland.
Tel: +353 1 4923333; Fax: +353 1 4922777
E-mail: books@obrien.ie
Website: www.obrien.ie
Reprinted 2007

ISBN: 978-1-84717-061-3
Text © copyright Eileen Bergin 2007
Photographs © copyright Denis Bergin 2007
Copyright for typesetting, editing,
layout and design © The O'Brien Press Ltd

Bergin, Eileen
The butler's pantry cookbook : recipes for all seasons
1. Cookery I. Title
641.5

2 3 4 5 6 7 8 9 10
07 08 09 10 11 12

Cover photograph by Jocasta Clarke
Cover photograph: chocolate fudge cake, recipe p. 134
Printed and bound by Grafo, S.A. – Bilbao, Spain.

CONTENTS ••••••••••••••••••••••••••

•••••••••• RECIPES
SPRING

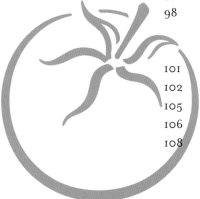

DEDICATION

To my parents Gerry and Pat for giving me such strong roots to grow from, wings to fly away and the most wonderful memories that I will cherish forever.

To my wonderful husband Denis, for his kindness, his unending support, his constant encouragement, his patience, his great photographs and his fantastic gin & tonics; I could not have done this book without him. To my sons Karl and Claus who have been brought up on The Butler's Pantry and have eaten our food from the day they were born; no wonder they are such fine, tall, good-looking chaps! To Jacquie, my partner, who has made my life so much easier and so much fun and who has adopted my dream as if it was her own. To my friends and colleagues all of whom have contributed so much over the last twenty years in different ways and have helped me achieve my dream. I thank you all from the bottom of my heart.

ACKNOWLEDGEMENTS

I would like to thank some amazing people who have given so much of their time, effort, expertise, knowledge, support and encouragement to me over the years and while doing this book. In no particular order: Anita Coleman, for being there; Margaret Davidson for her love and wonderful baking skills; Margaret Byrnes for understanding me and where I was going; Betty Kavanagh for working alongside me for fourteen years and loving our customers; Mary Moore, Yvonne Keating and Angela Doherty for their unfailing, long-term commitment to The Butler's Pantry; Ann Kenny for her sense of style and fun; Jocasta Clarke for her beautiful cover photograph.

I would also like to thank all the team at The O'Brien Press: Helen Carr, editor, Emma Byrne, designer, and Michael O'Brien who cajoled me into doing this book. I would like to thank all the fantastic people who work so hard at The Butler's Pantry both in the kitchens and in the shops, ensuring that our customers get real, fresh, wholesome food every day. I am so very proud of all of them and their commitment to delivering the very best. A business like ours needs to know that it can rely on its suppliers to deliver the very best quality all the time in order for us to do our job and I would like to thank all those suppliers who have done just that and have grown with us over the last twenty years. Food in Ireland has come a long way since The Butler's Pantry first opened its doors in 1987, due in no mean way to all the dedicated, professional, committed and passionate growers and producers who strive to deliver quality over quantity despite the odds and I thank them for keeping focused.

Finally a big thank you to all our customers who support us every day and whose opinions we value greatly. The Butler's Pantry would not be the same without you.

I just love food, buying it, preparing it, cooking it and thinking about it. Even as a small child I loved it. It's such a pity that I did not realise how much I loved it when I was young; if I had thought that I'd like a career with food I might have persuaded my parents to send me to some fantastic culinary institution to learn everything I could and have a proper apprenticeship while I was still in my teens, but I didn't, I was a late developer!

I am the eldest of seven children and my mother, who taught herself to cook after she got married, prepared and cooked three square family meals every day; by the time there were nine of us around the table, that was a lot of work and a great achievement by today's standards. Food was always delicious in our house – whether it was beans on toast (very nutritious), scrambled eggs, roast leg of lamb or steaks (now and again), we always looked forward to mealtimes.

My dad always made the French dressing at home whenever we had a green salad. It was slightly different every time because he was always trying to improve it. He would ask me to taste it to see if it needed more vinegar or French mustard or parsley or garlic, but each time it was delicious. Even with so many mouths to feed, especially for lunch during school time, Mum always had a proper meal and dessert ready. This was eaten very quickly as we only had an hour and a quarter and then we were gone back to school, leaving Mum to tackle the dishes and all of us ready to take on the world!

From a very early age I was helping in the kitchen or feeding the younger members of my family and without realising it I was becoming hooked on food

'COOKING IS LIKE LOVE, IT SHOULD BE ENTERED INTO WITH ABANDON OR NOT AT ALL.'

Harriet van Horne

and learning all the time. Sadly this tends not to happen as much anymore as people's lives have changed so completely; now, they are busy in a different way.

My mother often had to entertain up to sixteen people for dinner and she always wanted everything to be perfect — to look, smell and taste delicious, naturally! I was always involved in helping her on these occasions as were my other sisters after I left home.

Even when I was sent to boarding school I asked to be allowed to help in the school's kitchen and eventually Sister Murphy, who was very brave, relented and let me cook in the kitchen on Saturdays where I made curry for our evening meal!

As a family we left Dublin (and our shoes) behind us at the beginning of every summer and headed for Roundstone in the west of Ireland, an area we all loved passionately, and still do. We spent all our holidays beside the sea and I can still smell the seaweed and the salt. I always associate that smell with fishing for mackerel out in a boat, very early on a misty morning; once we had caught five

'THERE IS NO SUCH THING AS A LITTLE GARLIC.'

. . . .

or six of them we would head for home, clean the fish, dip them in a little seasoned flour and fry them quickly on a hot pan in a little butter and have them for breakfast with a squeeze of lemon and some fresh toast — heaven. We collected mussels from around the rocks and pools in buckets and brought them home to put straight into a large saucepan with water, wine, garlic, butter and parsley. They were served up, steaming hot, in big bowls with bread to mop up the juices. We caught flat fish on overnight lines, fried them in a little butter and had them with mashed potatoes.

The *pièces-de-résistances* were the big crabs that the fishermen threw up on the pier in the village and gave away to anyone who was brave enough to tackle them — imagine that today?

On Sundays we had a choice. We could have roast leg of lamb or roast leg of lamb or roast leg of lamb!! We choose roast leg of lamb, which we all looked forward to as it came with roast potatoes — and the parish priest, Fr Diskin, who always joined our family for Sunday lunch. It was compulsory to have fresh mint sauce and so one or two of us were sent off to fetch the mint which grew wild not far from where we lived. On arriving back it was quickly turned into the most delicious sauce. I use the same recipe today, and it only takes about five minutes to make.

One of our favourite suppers from those intoxicating summers was a salad made up of old-fashioned butterhead lettuces, cucumbers, Irish tomatoes, hard-boiled organic eggs, scallions, and fresh beetroot, most of which was grown locally, served with Heinz salad cream and home-made bread.

When I left school, not knowing what I wanted to do, I was packed off to study in France. Was I lucky or what?

I became exposed to some of the simplest and most beautiful food in the world and I ate it at every opportunity I got!

My friends and I used to treat ourselves to a meal out in Paris about once a month. We were all students and on a fixed income – practically nothing – and we loved going out and wandering into little restaurants and trying new foods. We feasted on great big salads tossed with bacon lardons and that creamy French vinaigrette that was just sharp enough to make your mouth water and your tongue tingle. Roast chicken with really crispy skin served with garlic potatoes and a green salad followed by a generous portion of chocolate mousse or a big wedge of oozing camembert and more French

'AND THE BEST BREAD WAS OF MY MOTHER'S MAKING – THE BEST IN ALL THE LAND'

baguette all served up as if we were the most important customers in the restaurant, and a pitcher of Beaujolais to wash it all down with. All of this simple, home-cooked, fresh, delectable food was ours for about four French francs each and we left those restaurants completely satisfied and happy with our lot. We definitely got value for money.

In hindsight, I realise that this was the continuation of my education and of my love affair with food. In the middle of the day I would leave class to get a bite to eat and it was usually a bowl of French onion soup slaked with brandy with a bread croute floating on the top and covered with grated gruyère or emmenthal cheese that became all stringy as you ate it. It was hot and filling and satisfied that basic requirement we all seek, comfort and warmth.

Sometimes I would have a plain omelette that was made in two seconds and brought to the table with a flourish along with a simple tomato salad or a slice of *pâté de campagne* served with some sliced gherkins and rustic country bread.

The simplicity and apparent ease with which these dishes were served was to stay with me forever and to influence my approach to food. It was a type of cooking based on very familiar ingredients that we all recognise. It was hearty and wholesome, full of honesty and generosity; in short it was real food.

While living, learning and loving in Paris I decided I could no longer beg, borrow or steal to survive and that I would have to get some sort of employment.

My first job was as a *monitrice de ski* in the high Alps on the east coast of France where in the early months of the year everything is snow-white, the skies are deep blue and the air is so sharp you can hear the bells that the goats and cattle wear around their necks tinkling in the distance. A *monitrice de ski* is someone who accompanies French children when they go on their annual skiing trips with their teachers where they have skiing in the mornings and classes in the afternoons.

'LOVE AND EGGS ARE BEST WHEN THEY ARE FRESH' — *Russian proverb*

Here in the Haute-Savoie I experienced food from a different region, like roast lamb with a potato and onion gratin, or lamb stew in white wine, a daube of beef, or sautéed veal with carrots. This was food to build us up and give us strength, as skiing is a strenuous sport and the fresh air gave us all terrific appetites. We were exposed to the various cheeses of the region as well as cold meats, saucisson, fresh fruit, compôtes, sweet pastries, and the most wonderful hot chocolate and steaming coffee with lots of hot milk. We would have chocolate cakes, lemon tarts, pear clafoutis and almond tart, and the thing about all this food was that nobody put on any weight. The food was real, no additives or preservatives, just local produce cooked simply and served simply.

I had the privilege of doing this job for a month at a time and when it was finally over I headed back to Paris in search of another assignment!

I decided I needed a better-paid and more permanent job in Paris to sustain my extra-curricular forays into the delights and temptations of French food.

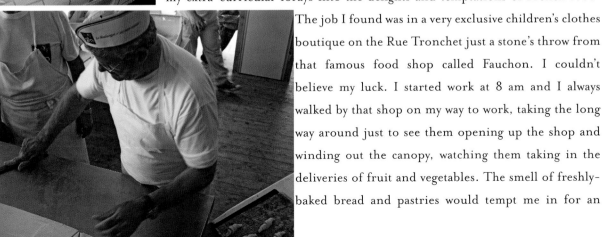

The job I found was in a very exclusive children's clothes boutique on the Rue Tronchet just a stone's throw from that famous food shop called Fauchon. I couldn't believe my luck. I started work at 8 am and I always walked by that shop on my way to work, taking the long way around just to see them opening up the shop and winding out the canopy, watching them taking in the deliveries of fruit and vegetables. The smell of freshly-baked bread and pastries would tempt me in for an almond croissant, which I really couldn't afford, but I couldn't afford to go without either. I would eat a third of it on the way to work and put the rest in my bag until halfway through the morning when I would sneak another third and finally at lunch-time after a tomato and mozzarella baguette with pesto I would have the third third!! Talk about rationing.

I learned then that it was not the quantity that you ate, but the quality. By the time I returned to my tiny flat after work I was exhausted, and a fresh green salad with shavings of parmesan cheese that I brought back from the mountains sustained me until the following morning. I firmly believe that it should be the quality of the food that matters and not the quantity. We should know everything we can about the food we eat, where it comes from, who reared it or grew it, what kind of life it had and how far it has travelled. We should be asking these questions whenever we shop. It is in our own best interests and those of our children and older relatives that we know as much as we can about the food we consume so that we can make informed choices and be responsible for our own well-being and that of our families.

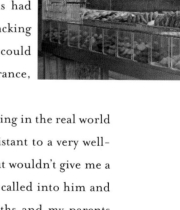

My time spent in the French capital and other regions had made an indelible impression on me and, on reluctantly packing my suitcase to return home, I put in as many memories as I could and as much cheese as would fit in between them and left France, but not for good.

On my return from France I had to find a job and start living in the real world and after endless searching I found a job as a personal assistant to a very well-known photographer in Dublin. He offered me the job, but wouldn't give me a start date!! I don't know how many times I phoned him or called into him and he kept putting me off until finally after about two months and my parents telling me I had imagined the 'offer', I arrived into his studio one morning at 9 am and said I was there to start work. I never looked back and after about two years with his company I was appointed company secretary, the youngest ever.

The work was exciting and different. I was dealing with public relations companies, photographers, big businesses, the government, the tourist board, ad agencies and so forth. Everybody wanted everything yesterday and this was long before digital cameras, digital photography and laptops. It took several hours to produce a black and white print and longer for colour prints. Little did I know that it was here I would meet my future husband. In fact we worked side by side in the business for a number of years and one day he asked me out to lunch and it wasn't very long after that that he asked me to marry him.

Shortly after getting married I started going to as many cookery schools as I could to learn as much as possible about food and how to cook it. I loved the Cordon Bleu Cookery School in London and Robert Carrier's cookery school at Hintlesham Hall in Ipswich. Anton Mosimann of The Dorchester Hotel in London eventually allowed me to spend time working in his kitchens because he probably realised it was the only way to get rid of me! And of course I spent many happy visits listening and learning from Darina Allen of Ballymaloe Cookery School in Cork.

'NOTHING GOOD WAS EVER ACHIEVED WITHOUT ENTHUSIASM' — *Ralph Waldo Emerson*

When my children were born, we moved to live in the country where I started giving cookery classes in my home. These enabled me to get to know my neighbours who were wonderful in their support and we had some very enjoyable years learning together. Once my boys started school, and help arrived in the form of a wonderful nanny, Margaret Davidson, I found myself out on the road and catering for companies in Dublin who entertained their clients in-house.

After a few years I knew I wanted something different – I knew I wanted to expose the public to real food. I felt the time was right to set up a small retail outlet and sell fresh, chilled, wholesome food, like I grew up with and enjoyed in France, to the public. There was no sector out there providing this option for people when they shopped for food and I felt very strongly that people needed a choice.

And so I headed for the States and Canada to see what they were doing and to get a feel for food to 'take home'. The Americans have always been very good at buying what they need to celebrate a wonderful occasion or to feed the family when just lazing about at the weekends, even barbeque food and salads are bought in, anything to make life easier for the cook!!

Women's lives there were increasingly busy and consumed by school runs, piano lessons, tennis and basketball, fund-raisers, concerts, the gym, going to the movies, supporting their husbands and probably working either full- or part-time as well; no wonder they didn't have time to cook! But they knew that they wanted good food for their families and so the culture of buying fresh, wholesome, tasty produce from stores that were aware of their needs had begun.

I could see this in all the food shops I visited on my two or three trips to the east coasts of America and Canada. There were wonderful bread shops that sold cakes and cookies, jams, marmalades and honey, breakfast cereals and juices. The fruit and vegetable shops were awe-inspiring — everything more or less ready to use. Lettuces were freshly washed and not sealed in bags like we have today, vegetables ready to cook and fruit that made your mouth water. And then … there was the deli, which for me was like being let loose in Paris all over again; fresh cheeses from all over the world, pâtés, terrines, fresh sauces to add to pasta or to cover ready-prepared meats to pop straight into the oven, along with cooked baby new potatoes, or roasties flavoured with rosemary or thyme and even dauphinoise potatoes. If it wasn't there you could order it — cold meats freshly sliced to go with a huge array of freshly prepared salads, foods ready to go on the barbeque and if you didn't want to do any work at all you could buy a great selection of meals to take home and put straight into the oven — I was convinced that it was only a matter of time before we in Ireland would want exactly the same thing.

And so I came home, my head bursting with ideas and started looking for my ideal shop. I didn't know then that I was starting something that was going to consume my life for the next twenty years, or that I was going to meet the most wonderful people along the journey or that I was going to learn so much, a lot of it the hard way. I didn't realise that I was going to miss out on my children's school years, nor was I going to have much of a social life for a long time. But I did have wonderful support from my husband, children and family who all helped out in some way or another either working in the shops or driving to deliver food to shops or customers, and in helping me test recipes at home in our kitchen where we cooked and tried everything before we cooked it for our customers. When I think about it now, my children were fantastic. They could describe a meal and what was in it to my customers from an early age, and they very often did if they were in the shop doing their homework waiting for me to take them home.

And so in 1987 The Butler's Pantry was born …

'DAILY JOGGING IS GOOD FOR THE HEART, SO ARE HUGGING AND KISSING'

THE BUTLER'S PANTRY STORY

I opened the first Butler's Pantry on Mount Merrion Avenue in November 1987. It was the tiniest, cutest shop, about 200 square feet in total, and we did everything here in front of our customers. It was friendly, warm and homely and the smells of the food we were cooking wafted up the avenue and persuaded people to come in. Initially people thought I was completely mad and that it wouldn't last six months but I knew it would, I was determined that it would, and now twenty years and eight shops later we are still here operating out of state-of-the-art kitchens, which are located in Bray, Co. Wicklow.

When we opened we cooked fresh bread and cookies every day, made delicious cakes and puddings and were always trying out new dishes on our stoves and literally packing and selling them to our customers from the pot, almost. People used to wait five or ten minutes while we piped mashed potato on top of the shepherd's pie or added sliced mushrooms and gherkins to the beef stroganoff or rolled up a roulade and they would go home happy in the knowledge that the food had just come 'out of the oven'. People used to say that it reminded them of their childhood.

Then the same customers came back in the following day and gave us a full report on what they had had for dinner the night before – instant customer feedback!

We got to know all our customers and their families, their problems, their pets, their likes and dislikes. We introduced them to familiar and new foods and encouraged them to try everything – they could taste before they bought. Slowly but surely they began to trust us, to look forward to what we cooked each day and to come in to us on the way home and take a new dish to try and so we learnt a lot together and guided each other. We listened to what they actually wanted. In those days very few people had allergies to food and ours had no additives or preservatives (and it still doesn't), but was prepared fresh every day with the very best ingredients I could get.

The Butler's Pantry opened in the mornings at nine am and seldom closed before nine or ten at night, and often we would be there until midnight – still open – though there were only two of us, or sometimes three. It was a wonderful time of learning, fear, anxiety, excitement, exhaustion, dreaming and planning

for the future (that was day to day) and making new friends with customers and suppliers, and trying with bank managers!! But it was never dull and I loved it passionately and still do.

It felt like a child that was growing up – slowly.

By 1992 our little shop on Mount Merrion Avenue was bursting at the seams and so my landlord, Jim McCabe, very kindly gave up his office behind my shop to allow me to expand my kitchen into what was no longer his boardroom. The builders arrived and knocked down the wall between the two and we got more space – fantastic – free to do more ...

It was about this time that I was persuaded by a wonderful lady called Betty Kavanagh, who had joined us in 1991, to purchase a till – up until then we had been operating out of a tin box underneath the counter until it was stolen one day from under our eyes. I think we were busy making roulades when it happened. And so very shortly after, Derek Leavy arrived, with our second-hand till in tow and we have never looked back. Derek is still looking after us today and I must say he has been wonderful, always there for us.

With the extra space came extra people and overheads and so in 1992 I decided to open a second outlet in Donnybrook and to service it from our kitchen on Mount Merrion Avenue. For this I needed transport, other than my own car, and so I invested in a secondhand little red Peugeot van with our name on the side. I thought I'd died and gone to heaven; I now had my own fleet.

And so we delivered every day from Blackrock to Donnybrook. We catered in Dublin for big and busy companies, we did dinner parties in people's homes, we did christenings, birthdays, anniversaries and, unhappily, sad occasions too, we said 'yes' to everybody and learnt a lot

'To LOVE WHAT YOU DO AND TO FEEL THAT IT MATTERS, HOW COULD ANYTHING BE MORE FUN?' – *Katherine Graham*

along the way. And all the time we were doing more and more food in our kitchens for customers to take home and enjoy.

By 1996 enough was enough – we were now producing hundreds of meals a day, lots of soups, sandwiches and cookies and we had a full time bakery and no room!! Unfortunately we could not go out to one of the industrial estates on the outskirts of the city and take a large commercial unit as the rents were enormous and the distance from our shops was way too far for deliveries – we would spend most of the time in traffic, and so I looked closer to home and found a premises just two miles away from our first shop which was to solve our immediate space problem. I split our kitchens in two, keeping the bakery/cookies (and delicious smells) at the back of our Mount Merrion Avenue shop and moving the production of our meals and catering to our new kitchen at the back of our new shop in Temple Hill in Monkstown. Now we had delicious smells in two locations and a third shop, which I was determined would pay its own way. Eleven years and a lot of meals later it is still more than paying its own way and it's a wonderful little outpost all on its own, but today the kitchen is no longer there.

The business, at this stage, was growing very quickly and there was great demand for what we were doing and it occurred to me that I might be able to facilitate our customers even more by having The Butler's Pantry product (meals) in other, very good, independent retailers and owner/manager shops. So I approached a number of nice food shops and asked if they would take the product – frozen as opposed to fresh and therefore they would have no waste problems and we would have no returns – everyone was happy and so the wholesale side of the business was born. After all these years we are still supplying some of our earliest customers who have been wonderfully supportive of us.

At this time we were still writing all our labels out by hand and so we investigated the possibility of having a printed sleeve made to slide over our product with the relevant information printed on it. I still remember the first day these arrived, everyone was thrilled, no more writing for hours. We were getting posher all the time!

By 1998 our little red secondhand Peugeot van was due to retire and we bought our first brand new white van with our 'logo' written all over it. The Butler's Pantry was really booming and I had about twenty-five terrific people working with me at this time. I knew the potential was there to take the business nationwide and that I could replicate what we were doing in Dublin in other parts of the country. Besides, having worked so very hard to get the business to this level I really wanted to secure its future and so I started to be on the look out for someone as mad and as passionate as I was to join my team and help me take it to the next level. This search took two years before I found a terrific partner, but I was lucky and in 2000 I met Jacquie Marsh, who happened to be looking for a project to get

NIALL HILL

'NOTHING IS REALLY WORK UNLESS YOU'D RATHER BE DOING SOMETHING ELSE' — *George Halas*

her teeth into and who joined The Butler's Pantry. Her background was marketing and brand development along with business excellence. There was no stopping us after that. She wasn't a year in the place and we had a computerised labelling machine!

In 2001 we moved into a bigger space in Bray where we had our main kitchen, keeping the bakery in Mount Merrion Avenue.

Our executive chef and Director of Food, Niall Hill joined us in 2001.

Niall had nine years experience working and teaching in Canada before he returned to Ireland to take up the position of head chef at the famed Rathsallagh House Hotel in Naas. He brought insight, calm, generosity of spirit and loads of knowledge with him and is today a wonderful inspiration to all his colleagues who work with him in his kitchen.

In 2001 we broke the 1 million euro turnover and every penny we made we ploughed back into the business. In 2003/2004 we were the recipients of the Bord Bia 'Small Business of the Year' Award, which thrilled us all. In the same year we revamped two of our shops, namely Merrion Avenue and Donnybrook, giving them a more modern look and feel.

Up until now the colours of the shops had been burgundy and so we changed to slick black and white and a great red.

In January 2004 having looked for two years for another shop we found Sandymount, a tiny little shop looking out onto the green in the village. It's a great location and we love it and all the new and wonderful customers we met when we opened. Sometimes the older shops gave out to us if a new shop took one or two of the old customers away and so an element of competition started between the shops which created a buzz. It took us just two weeks to get Sandymount ready to open to the public. Then we were on the trail again and found our first shop on the north side of the city in Clontarf, at 2 Vernon Avenue.

This was a big project. We divided the premises in two and my brother Brian took one half and opened a fish deli/tapas bar and The Butler's Pantry took the other half.

This was the first time we acquired the services of an architect, Patrick Power, to help us launch a 'new look' shop which was a great size, so much so that we put a cookery demonstration kitchen at the back of the shop where I give cookery classes nearly every month. This was a really great way to talk to the new customers who came in to the shop to see what we were about and to taste the

THE BUTLERS PANTRY.

Our Promise

"Natural Ingredients, delicious recipes, hand prepared... From our kitchen to Yours"

EOIN WARNER

food. This shop was the first to have automatic sliding doors and it will be the last as they drive everyone mad!!!

We were getting good at opening shops; we now had five. We were also concentrating on our kitchens and on getting production levels up without affecting the quality of our product. I did not want us to make huge batches of anything. We continued to make the same size batches. If we needed more food we just cooked another batch, so keeping the quality and integrity of the product.

Life was never dull. We had plenty of ideas and plans and we were constantly revisiting them. In 2005 we won the Small Firms Association 'Retailer of the Year', which was further recognition of all our hard work. Also that year our sixth shop opened in another village. This time in Rathgar, which is a lovely, leafy suburb of Dublin; once again we are situated in the village, across from the church, with huge big windows looking out onto the street where we can see people coming and going all day.

We launched our presence on the internet, at www.thebutlerspantry.ie, with the help of Lynda Shepherd who had some terrific ideas for a friendly and informative site

At this point in time it is not too difficult for us to open for business in a new area because The Butler's Pantry name is very well-known and is synonymous with great quality food and service. We are so very lucky to have this reputation, but we have all worked very hard for it and we guard it zealously.

At this stage we still had two kitchens producing all the food, and both Jacquie and I had been searching hard for a premises to put both the kitchens into under one roof at last.

Eventually (and when we were nearly giving up hope) we found two units for sale in Bray, not too many miles away from where we were. We knew we had to buy them, but with what we did not know; we couldn't afford to let that stop us. With the help of our financial controller, Margaret Byrnes, a wonderful bank, IIB, and two understanding husbands we raised the necessary funds to enable us to put a noose around our necks and become the proud owners of the premises that was to become kitchens for all sections of the business at long last. The Butler's Pantry had finally found a permanent home.

Our architect was duly roped in to do the plans, which grew and developed the more conversations we had and the wonderful extra space that we had just acquired started to fill up with everyone's priorities. We lived by budgets, but eventually in April of 2006 we moved in.

Eoin Warner, who joined us in 2003, was trained at Shannon and came from the famed Gleneagles Hotel in Scotland. He was appointed Head of Retail at The Butler's Pantry and joined Jacquie, Niall and myself on the board of directors in November 2006. Eoin's love of and abiding passion for food are evident in all he does in The Butler's Pantry.

All our shops are committed to supporting local charities in their area enabling us, The Butler's Pantry, to give something back to the community who support us throughout the year. Today we employ over seventy people of many nationalities. Each and every one of them contributes enormously to the ethos and essence that is The Butler's Pantry and we would be lost without them. I hope that I have achieved some of what I set out to do and that I have ensured the continued growth of what is an amazing business.

'WHEN LOVE AND SKILL WORK TOGETHER, EXPECT A MASTERPIECE' — *John Ruskin*

WHY SEASONALITY MATTERS

REAL FOOD COMES FROM THE EARTH WITH CLAY ON IT AND NOT FROM PLASTIC BAGS!!

I feel that because our lives are so hectic we have become accustomed to doing a 'supermarket shop' once a week, to save time, to be able to get everything under the one roof, to have choice and maybe even to get ideas. We can park our car for very little, go to the ATM machine if necessary, get our hair done and pick up the dry-cleaning on the way out and I agree that it's a very attractive and handy proposition. The dreaded shop is done and dusted for another week. We have become used to this way of life, but now we are being asked to look at what the real cost of all this convenience might be.

It's hard to believe that because we no longer buy onions from the farmer in the next county and carrots, locally grown, in the vegetable shop and potatoes from the weekly farmers' market, our local communities are dying, the post

'TELL ME WHAT YOU EAT AND I WILL TELL YOU WHAT YOU ARE' –
Anthelme Brillat-Savarin, French Gourmet & Lawyer, 1755-1826 • • • • • • • • • • • • • • • • • • •

ALLAN McGOVERN OF NEWFRESH
WITH EILEEN BERGIN

office is disappearing, the bank is moving to a bigger town and there are no jobs for young people in the areas they grew up in — why? We have to look at our supermarket trolley. We probably have tomatoes from Holland, raspberries and blueberries from the USA, peppers from Israel, garlic from France, and chicken from Holland or England, lemons from Peru and so on. Clearly, we cannot grow all of this produce in Ireland as our climate isn't hot enough (not yet), but there is a lot of food that can be grown at the right time and in season; this in the long run would be far better for all of us.

The larger supermarkets source a great amount of the produce we buy from them throughout the world in order to give us a feeling of huge choice, well-being and familiarity. In actual fact they are adding hugely to the air miles necessary to transport the produce to our stores and to our tables, and so contributing to the environmental damage and the carbon footprint that we keep hearing about on a daily basis, which we as consumers are going to have to pay for in the long run.

By looking for food that is grown neither in our own country nor locally we are reducing our ability to feed ourselves as a nation. What would we do if we had another world war and could no longer import food into our country, but had to rely on our food producers to feed us — where would they come from? Surely it is very short-sighted to think they could reappear overnight when we so callously deserted them for seemingly better pastures.

When we don't support our own farmers, they stop farming because they can't earn a decent living; when we don't support our local greengrocer, they close down because they can't pay their mortgage; when we don't shop in our local butcher's, suddenly we don't have a butcher anymore because they can no longer compete with the supermarkets.

Not only has our local fishmonger disappeared, but a huge selection of our fish stocks are either threatened or extinct because our waters have been over fished in order to provide a year-round supply. The closer to home our food is grown the more seasonal it will be.

Village or community life as we once knew it has all but disappeared and with it our ability to be self-sufficient, to provide good local employment and to be masters of our own destiny. But I think we have nearly come full circle, not so much by choice, but by being made aware of what's happening to our environment and by asking ourselves what we can do to improve it.

One of the areas we can start to make a difference is by using our purchasing power when we shop. If we know that the food we are buying is in season, that is, grown at a time that nature intended and not forced or fed with chemicals, we will benefit enormously from the freshness, the good taste and the greater well-being.

If we can take a little time to look at the labels on the food we buy to see the origin of these foods we can make a choice – Irish tomatoes as opposed to Dutch, herbs from Wicklow instead of Israel, onions from Cork instead of Spain, and so on. Our purchases will influence the big supermarkets eventually. Take, for example, the choice of organic fruit and vegetables when they first arrived in the shops. The supermarkets had a tiny selection, but as customers began demanding more of this product the supermarkets had to increase the supply; as we create more demand for Irish produce and buy fewer imported products, the supermarkets will have to re-think their strategy – so we can make a difference, but we have to persevere. Little by little we can incorporate changes in our daily diet without too much hardship and every little helps.

I hope this gives you the confidence when you shop to look out for these items and to see where they come from and if they are not Irish to ask why not.

One of the things that excites me greatly is the huge upsurge in Farmers' Markets that is evident all around the country. I would urge you to try to support these amazing people and their produce; they, against all the odds, struggle with the bureaucracy that surrounds producing food that does not fall into the conventional mainstream.

We are the ones who will benefit in the long run. Being able to talk to the grower of your fruit and vegetables, to the producers of fantastic cheeses and dairy produce and to the farmer who rears his own pigs for bacon and sausages – all of this food, along with breads, sauces and chocolate produced lovingly and carefully by hand not too far from where you live – is very reassuring. To know the source of the food you buy encourages awareness, community spirit and a wonderful lesson in geography (in Ireland) for our children, most of whom think that food comes from the supermarket!

With our support these producers will flourish and we are ensuring the continued access to fresh, wholesome and local produce for the future.

DON'T BE AFRAID OF THE KITCHEN

The kitchen is the heart of the home; it's where everything happens, it's where you go first thing in the morning to make breakfast, it's where you sit and have a cup of tea when everyone has rushed out to work, it's where you put the kettle on when you're halfway through the housework. Even those of us who spend all day away from our homes like to come home and put the kettle on, or start making or putting together a simple meal for the rest of the family who, after a busy day, will find comfort and familiarity in coming to the kitchen. Is it any wonder that the kitchen is probably the most important room in the house?

As such, your kitchen should be warm and cosy, bright and clean, with plenty of space and surface area to work and play in. At the same time it is important that it is not cluttered, nor the surfaces completely full of items you don't use as this will put you off actually preparing and cooking food. Have a home for everything. Keep your food processor or food mixer out on top along with a weighing scales, have somewhere you can roll out pastry, made or bought, a bread bin, a toaster, and somewhere to chop vegetables. If you have easy access to these items you are more likely to use them than if they are hidden at the back of a press where you don't see them.

One of the best additions I ever made to my own kitchen was an 'InSinkErator' – it grinds up everything (except onion skins) and reduces the amount of waste we put in the bin. But this is something that can be put into a kitchen if and when you decide to give it a face-lift in the future.

In this day and age so many of us are saying 'no' to a formal dining room and having a larger kitchen with a dedicated dining area and even a sitting area also which means, more than ever, that all the action is taking place in the kitchen!

There are a few essentials that every kitchen should have: invest in some good stainless steel pans (with heavy bottoms!!) a small and a large non-stick frying pan, a small, medium and large bowl in Pyrex or stainless steel, a measuring jug, some wooden spoons, an electric whisk, some small sharp knives and a good carving set, a set of measuring spoons and a set of American cup measures (as a lot of recipes today use cup, metric and imperial until we all get used to metric), a swivel vegetable peeler and a selection of baking tins. With all of this paraphenalia you will be able to tackle most things; in fact you could survive on a lot less.

If you have an area you feel comfortable cooking in, either beside the cooker or at a special worktop, try to have the basics — like olive oil, sea salt and pepper mill, flour, sugar and eggs — to hand, as this will save you walking miles and wasting time. If you are going to make a dish from a recipe read it well first and then assemble all the ingredients you need before you start. Never tackle a new dish when you are under pressure or very tired as very often it won't turn out right and you will be frustrated and annoyed. It's better to have a few reliable recipes that you can put together for meals during the week and try new ones at the weekends or when you have time. Remember to clean as you go. Try washing pots and pans, spoons and bowls and cleaning around the cooker and your work area before you sit down to eat. It is so nice to look at a clean, tidy kitchen when you are enjoying your meal and you will feel less like cleaning up after dinner. It is also good practice for when you have friends in to dinner if you are eating in the kitchen as you don't want them to see all your hard work except when they taste the food!

The kitchen is probably one of the most 'nurturing' rooms because it has atmosphere and warmth. It is a wonderful place to share preparing meals and setting a table to suit the occasion. Even on week nights when we are all very busy it is nice to be able to sit down together and share the day's experiences over a simple meal. Whether it be a bowl of soup and an omelette, a casserole and rice, or a quiche and a salad, it's the sharing and the conviviality and the discussion about the food and the eventual clean plates that satisfies an inner craving and bonds us together.

For those of us who are not born attached to our kitchens or cookers, working in them can be a daunting experience and I want to assure you that it needn't be. I want to encourage you to try the recipes in this book, and if at first you don't succeed try again! It is such a rewarding achievement both for you and the recipients of your love and attention, and with each successful foray into the kitchen you'll be encouraged to continue trying new recipes and building up your repertoire and before you know it you will be a wonderful cook!

'AFTER A GOOD DINNER, ONE CAN FORGIVE ANYBODY, EVEN ONE'S OWN RELATIONS' — *Oscar Wilde*

STORE CUPBOARD BASICS

Cooking at home is something we all seem to be doing less and less of as we try to juggle busy working and family lives. There don't seem to be enough hours in the day to do everything and yet still find time to cook after a busy day at the office or running around with our children, getting them to and from school, sports, homework and so on. Because we have become so 'time poor' we find it easier to buy something frozen or from a tin or a packet and, while this makes a nice change from time to time, it is no substitute for the real pleasure of good food.

If we can have the 'basics' in our cupboards at home it is a little easier to put together some quick meals in minutes.

SUGGESTIONS

Eggs, organic or free-range, for omelettes and frittatas

butter

Stork margarine, for pastry

unsalted butter, for some recipes, although normal butter is a good substitute

Kallo stock cubes, (organic preferably, although any good quality stock cubes will do, or you can make your own)

crackers, for a lunchtime or after school snack with cheese/tomatoes/tapenade on top

digestive biscuits, also great with cheese and as a base for cheesecakes

various flours, plain or cream flour, self-raising, wholemeal & strong for making bread

mustards, English & French, a definite for making French dressings

chocolate, Bourneville or Green & Black's 70% cocoa, to make simple chocolate mousse & sauce for ice-cream

couscous, makes a great salad to go with barbeque food

extra virgin olive oil & sunflower oil

chilli sauce, for barbeques

Worcestershire sauce, for Bloody Mary soup & sausages

honey, for health & for some French dressings

Bonne Maman jam, for trifle & breakfast

Maldon sea salt, to use every day instead of table salt, (you will use less)

coarse ground black pepper, for everything

marmalade, Bonne Maman or buy 'Homecook' & make your own, very satisfying

brazil nuts, hazelnuts & almonds, for muesli, in meringues, on cereals

porridge oats, the quickest & most nutritious breakfast ever

pasta, lots of it! the quickest supper ever

parmesan cheese, buy Parmigiano Reggiano in a chunk & serve at the table with a grater

red & white wine vinegar & balsamic vinegar, great for salad dressings,

mint sauce

rice, basmati, brown, Thai & red rice, for when you don't feel like peeling potatoes

tinned chickpeas, for making hummus

tinned cannellini beans

tinned, chopped tomatoes, a fantastic standby for soups & sauces

tinned tomato purée

tinned baked beans, quick & nutritious suppers – just add sausages

coconut milk, for curries & queen of pudding

brown & white sugars, try to buy unrefined

cheeses, good strong cheddar, a blue cheese, soft goats' cheese & parmesan

chutney, mango to go with curries or coronation chicken

diced bacon, can be bought in the supermarket in little packets, great with pasta & coq-au-vin

frozen peas in the freezer, for soup, risotto & pasta

cold meats like **cured ham, salami & proscuitto**, all are available in supermarkets & have a good shelf life

It is necessary to have onions, carrots, potatoes, lettuce, tomatoes, but you will have to purchase these every week or as you need them as they are perishable.

With all these basics in your pantry, you could make the most fantastic food at very short notice and not a preservative or additive in sight.

Get shopping!!

W hen it comes to cooking, it's like any other activity or sport that you might wish to learn. If you know the basics you can do an awful lot; that's why I have included this section to give you a few easy 'building blocks' that will enable you to finalise the new dishes that you are going to try!!

So ... work that store cupboard and use the basics to accompany the recipes in this book to enhance the simplest of meals.

I really hope you find them useful.

Happy cooking!

PARSLEY OR BASIL PESTO

SERVES 4-6,
ADDED TO PASTA

1 oz / 25g fresh parsley or basil (one or the other, not both)

1 or 2 cloves garlic, finely chopped

2 oz / 50g freshly grated parmesan (Reggiano Parmigiano)

1 oz / 25g pine kernels

3 fl. oz / 75ml extra virgin olive oil

pinch sea salt

METHOD

Put all the ingredients except the oil and salt into a food processor. Whizz together for a second or two and add the oil and a pinch of salt. Taste and correct the seasoning. This will keep in the fridge for a few weeks – keep covered and bring to room temperature before using. A blob of this is great on minestrone soup or mixed in with hot pasta or served on top of grilled chicken or fish. It is also nice spread on bruschetta topped with some sliced, Irish cherry tomatoes with a sliver of parmesan cheese on top.

SALAD SPLASH

SERVES 4-6
(DRESSED LEAVES)

This is a fantastic stand-by to have in a jar in the fridge, although it can be put together in less than 5 minutes provided you have all the basics in the store cupboard!

4 tbsps extra virgin olive oil

1 tbsp balsamic vinegar, preferably aged 5-10 years

a pinch of sea salt

1/4 tsp caster sugar

1/4 tsp dried chilli flakes

1/4 tsp garlic salt

1/4 tsp white pepper

METHOD

Put the five dry ingredients into a bowl and add the olive oil and then the balsamic vinegar. Whisk together to help the sugar dissolve and bring the oil and vinegar together. Drizzle over your salad leaves just before serving.

The salad leaves must not be dressed until just before serving otherwise the leaves become soggy and limp.

FRENCH DRESSING

SERVES 4-6,
DRESSED LEAVES

2 fl. oz / 55ml white wine vinegar

5 fl. oz / 150ml sunflower oil

1 tsp grainy honey-mustard

1 tsp runny honey

1 clove of garlic, finely chopped

4 tsps finely-chopped parsley

sea salt & ground white pepper

METHOD

Put all the ingredients into a food blender and blend for 1 or 2 minutes. Put into a screw top jar and keep in the fridge until needed.

Bring back to room temperature and shake the jar well before drizzling over salad leaves. Serve immediately. Salad leaves must not be dressed until just before serving as they will become soggy and limp.

BACON & CHEDDAR CHEESE LOAF

SERVES 4–6,
8 SLICES

This is a delicious loaf that can be rustled up at very short notice and all kinds of things can be used to ring the changes! It goes beautifully with soup or salads and only takes about 10 minutes to put together and 25 minutes to cook.

a little butter, for greasing

4 streaky bacon rashers, chopped, or a box of lardons (available in supermarkets)

10 oz / 275g plain flour

1 level tbsp baking powder

1 tsp sea salt

pinch of English mustard

2 oz / 50g mature cheddar, grated or in tiny cubes

1 large egg

8 fl. oz / 225 ml milk, plus 1 tbsp extra

2–3 tbsp chopped fresh parsley

METHOD

Pre-heat the oven to 200° C / 400° F / gas 6.

Grease the base and sides of a 450g / 1 lb loaf tin and line the base with baking parchment. Snip the bacon into strips, dry-fry in a pan until a little crisp and then cool. Meanwhile put the flour, baking powder, salt and mustard powder into a bowl and stir. Add the cheese, bacon, egg, 8 fl. oz / 225 ml milk and the parsley. Stir well with a wooden spoon until it has a soft, dropping consistency – add extra milk if needed. Spread in the tin and bake for 25 minutes until risen, golden brown and firm to the touch. You can serve it immediately, but it will be a little hard to cut – try to let it cool a little beforehand.

It's really very good!

GRAVY

SERVES 4-6

Making gravy should not be a traumatic event and yet many think that it is! This gravy can be made when cooking any roast meat as you need the meat juices for the gravy.

a sprinkling of plain flour, about 1 tsp, (optional)

2 fl. oz / 55ml red or white wine

5-10 fl. oz / 150-275ml organic beef / chicken stock, or water

1 tsp dark brown sugar

sea salt & freshly-ground black pepper, to season

METHOD

Remove the meat from the roasting tin. Tilt the roasting tin to one side and drain off the excess oil or fat, leaving only the sedimenty juices from the meat. Return the roasting tin to the hob, and keep warm over a moderate heat. If you like your gravy slightly thickened, add about a teaspoon of flour to the tin and blend the flour into the nice meaty bits in the roasting tin with a wooden spoon; cook for a minute or two until brown. This also helps to cook the flour through. Add 5-10 fl.oz of stock and blend well with the flour. It may be necessary to use a whisk to make sure you have no lumps in the gravy. Bring to the boil and allow to simmer for two to three minutes. Add a teaspoon of dark brown sugar and 2 fl. oz red or white wine, stir well together, bring to the boil and then simmer for one minute. Check the seasoning and strain into a jug.

Alternatively, without the flour, drain the fat from the roasting tin, return to the hob and heat for two to three minutes. Add the red or white wine and scrape all the tasty bits in the bottom of the tin into the wine, allow to reduce by half then add the stock or water, bring to the boil and simmer for one to two minutes. Add a teaspoon of brown sugar and blend well. Check the seasoning and strain the gravy into a jug or sauceboat and keep warm until ready to serve.

ROSEMARY ROASTIES

SERVES 4

These potatoes are fantastic served with almost everything and they take no time to cook. You could use other herbs if you are not a rosemary fan, such as thyme, bay, oregano or sage.

2 lbs / 900g old potatoes

3-4 tbsps extra virgin olive oil

a few sprigs rosemary

I or 2 cloves garlic, chopped (optional)

Maldon sea salt (if possible) & freshly-ground pepper

non-stick frying pan

METHOD

Peel and wash the potatoes and dry very well in a tea towel.

Cut into small dice and season with salt and pepper. Heat the olive oil in a non-stick pan over a high heat and when hot add in the potatoes and the rosemary. Reduce the heat to medium and cook for about 20 minutes, tossing every now and then, but not too often otherwise they won't get nice and brown. Towards the end of cooking time add the chopped garlic (if using) and mix with the potatoes taking care not to let it burn; add more oil if necessary. Serve in a hot dish with sprigs of rosemary on top.

Alternatively, you can start the potatoes on top of hob and then put the pan or oven dish into a hot oven and continue to cook them in the same way for about 15 to 20 minutes.

GRATIN DAUPHINOIS

SERVES 6

This is the ultimate potato dish; it's so good that you would eat it by itself although it is great with steaks, pork, roast lamb or beef in fact with anything!!

1 kg / 2/1/2 lb potatoes, e.g. King Edwards, maris piper, desirée

1 clove of garlic, crushed, peeled & finely chopped

110g /4 oz butter

20 fl. oz / 600ml single cream

sea salt & freshly ground black pepper

110g / 4 oz gruyere, emmenthal or cheddar cheese, grated

METHOD

Heat the oven to 160° C / 325° F / gas mark 3.

Peel the potatoes and slice them finely using a mandolin or a food processor. Dry the slices very well to remove excess starch with a clean tea-towel or kitchen paper. Rub a large shallow ovenproof dish with half the garlic clove and a little of the butter. Put the remaining butter with the cream in a large saucepan and bring just to the boil. Finely dice what's left of the garlic and add it to the butter and cream along with the seasoning and the potato slices. Gently simmer for 8 minutes. Transfer to the prepared dish, spread out evenly and top with the gruyere and a little more seasoning. Bake for an hour and a half. Serve piping hot.

REALLY YUMMY MASHED POTATO

SERVES 4-5

2 lbs / 900g old potatoes, peeled

10 fl. ozs / 300ml milk

1-2 ozs / 25g-50g butter

sea salt & white pepper, to taste

METHOD

Cut the potatoes in half so that they are all about the same size.

Put the potatoes into a saucepan, cover with cold water, add a pinch of salt and bring to the boil. Lower the heat and allow the potatoes to cook gently until soft. Drain off the water immediately leaving none in the bottom of the pan. Return to a low heat and add the milk. Mash together with a potato masher to a nice soft consistency.

Add some or all of the butter and season with sea salt and ground white pepper.

These mashed potatoes will keep very well, covered, over a low heat or in a warm oven for at least an hour. So you don't have to do them at the last minute! It is very easy to transform the above 'yummy mash' to a different 'yummy mash'; simply add a bunch of chopped scallions to the mash to make champ, or a clove or two of finely-chopped garlic to make garlic mash. You could even add finely-chopped herbs like chives, parsley or fresh basil to the basic mash, or grainy honey mustard and suddenly you have four or five more accompaniments to add to your repertoire!

BRAISED PEAS & CARROTS — FRENCH STYLE

SERVES 8

1 oz / 25g butter

small bunch of spring onions

1 lb / 450g chantenay or baby carrots, halved lengthways

7 fl. oz / 200ml vegetable or chicken stock

1 lb / 450g frozen peas

1 romaine lettuce, shredded

METHOD

Melt the butter in a large saucepan over a medium heat. Add the sliced spring onions and cook for 2 to 3 minutes until softened. Add the carrots and stock and stir well. Bring to the boil then reduce the heat and simmer for a couple of minutes. Add the peas and the lettuce and cook for a further 4 minutes until the carrots are tender. Season to taste and serve with lamb, or any dish really, as this is a delicious combination and is very light.

EASY-PEASY PASTRY

SERVES 4-5,
MAKES AN 8"/20CM
TART OR QUICHE

This is the most versatile pastry ever and so easy to make. It can be used for either sweet or savoury dishes by just adding a teaspoon of caster or icing sugar. This quantity will make an 8" / 20cm apple tart or line a 8"-10" / 20cm quiche dish.

Tip: If you are using a mixer without a cover make sure to put a clean tea towel over the mixer to prevent the flour and bits of margarine flying around your kitchen!!

7 oz / 200g plain flour

5 oz / 150g margarine

pinch of sea salt

1 egg

METHOD

Put all the ingredients into a food mixer or processor and whiz together for 2 to 3 minutes until the mixture comes together. Remove from the mixer and roll out on a lightly-floured board to the size you require. Make sure to lightly grease the plate you are using or the quiche dish before lining with the pastry. This pastry can be made in advance, wrapped in greaseproof paper and cling film and kept in the fridge for 1 or 2 days. Bring back to room temperature before rolling out.

CHOCOLATE CHIP & ORANGE LOAF

SERVES 4–6,
8 SLICES

This is such a simple cake to make and can be put together in a few minutes. It uses no butter, but sunflower oil instead and is really light, moist and orangey.

8 oz / 225g self-raising flour

4 oz / 110g caster sugar

rind of 1 orange

5 fl. oz / 150ml orange juice

2 eggs

3 tbsps sunflower oil

4 oz / 110g chocolate chips

METHOD

Pre-heat the oven to 180° C / 350° F / gas 4.

Grease and base line a 900g/ 2 lb loaf tin. Sieve the flour and the caster sugar into a mixing bowl and stir in the orange rind. In a separate bowl, beat together the orange juice, eggs and sunflower oil. When well-blended, add to the dry ingredients. Gently stir until all the ingredients are combined. Finally, stir in the chocolate chips. Transfer to the prepared tin and bake for about 45 minutes or until a skewer or knife comes out clean.

Leave to sit in the tin for about 10 minutes then turn out onto a wire tray to go completely cold. You could drizzle melted chocolate over the top of the cake for a more 'posh' finish, but maybe simple is better!

SPRING

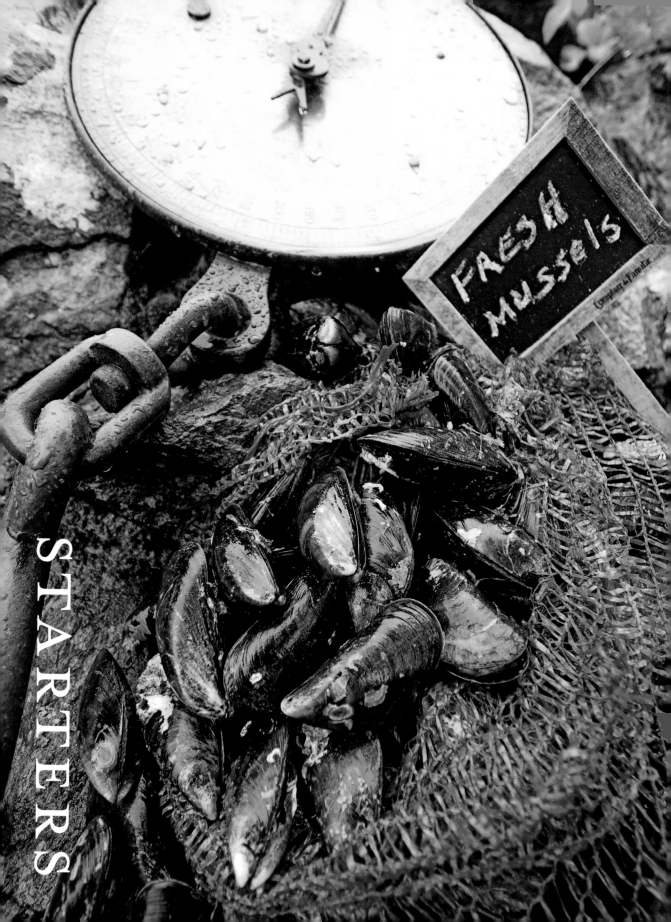

STARTERS

MARVELLOUS MUSSELS

SERVES 6

This is one of my favourite 'finger' food meals that we used to eat very often during the springs and summers in the west of Ireland when we would all go collecting mussels around the rocks and pools. Later on when I went to study in France it became even more delicious because they were a great source of inexpensive meals out served with a green salad and lots of French crusty bread to mop up all the juices.

2 tbsps of olive oil

2 oz / 50g butter

1 onion finely chopped, optional

1 or 2 cloves of garlic, peeled and finely chopped

3 lb / 1.4kg mussels, cleaned, washed & beards removed

7 1/2 fl.oz / 200ml dry white wine

sea salt & freshly-ground black pepper

2 bay leaves

1 cup finely-chopped parsley

METHOD

Heat the butter and olive oil in a large saucepan over a low heat.

Add the onion and garlic and cook for a few minutes, taking care not to let them brown. Add the mussels, wine, seasoning and bay leaves and bring to the boil. Cover and cook them for about 8 to 10 minutes until the mussel shells open. Shake the pan from side to side for a minute or two to ensure that all the mussels have opened and discard any that have not. Add the chopped parsley and serve immediately in a large heated bowl or in individual bowls. Have lots of crusty bread to mop up the lovely juices and serve a green salad on the side.

SWEETCORN & PRAWN SOUP

SERVES 2

This soup is very low in fat, and looks pretty served in nice bowls.

I onion, finely chopped

olive oil or sunflower oil

I potato, peeled & finely chopped

10 oz / 275g frozen sweetcorn

24 fl. oz / 750ml chicken or vegetable stock

7 oz / 200g peeled prawns

a small handful of chopped, fresh coriander

sea salt & pepper, to season

METHOD

In a large, non-stick pan, fry the onion with a little oil until soft. Add the potato and sweetcorn and season well. Add the stock and bring to the boil. Cook for ten minutes and then add the prawns and bring back to the boil.
Stir in the coriander and serve.

SMOKED SALMON & TROUT TIMBALES

SERVES 4-6

1-2 large, thin slices of smoked salmon per portion

4 oz / 110g smoked trout, without bones or skin

1 tbsp horseradish

1 oz / 25g butter, softened

1 tbsp lemon juice

approx 5 fl. oz / 150ml cream

sea salt & pepper to season, and flat-leaf parsley to garnish

METHOD

Put the smoked trout, horseradish, lemon juice and seasoning in the food processor and whizz together for 2 to 3 minutes. Scrape down the sides of the bowl and very slowly add the cream. Check for taste and adjust seasoning if necessary. A little pinch of cayenne pepper is sometimes nice added at this stage to give piquancy!

(This pâté is delicious eaten like this on brown bread or toast or alternatively makes a great simple dinner party starter.)

Line 4 to 6 ramekin dishes with cling film and then line with thin slices of smoked salmon, allowing it to overhang the dish.

Spoon in the trout pâté to about three-quarter way up the dish and then fold over the overhanging pieces of salmon and the cling film. Keep in the fridge until ready to eat, then turn out onto a plate and remove the cling film. The timbales can be made the day before you need them, or on the day, but they do benefit from a few hours in the fridge.

Serve with cucumber relish, which is wonderful with cold meats, smoked fish, hamburgers (homemade!), sandwiches and cheese. It keeps for weeks and weeks in the fridge.

CUCUMBER RELISH ·····················

2 lbs / 900g cucumbers, unpeeled and thinly sliced

2 small red onions thinly sliced

12 ozs / 350g sugar

1 tbsp sea salt

8 fl.ozs / 225 ml cider or white wine vinegar

dill, optional

METHOD

Mix the cucumber and onion in a large bowl. Add the sugar, salt and vinegar
and mix well to combine; this may seem like a lot of sugar, but it's necessary to
give it that 'sweet & sour' flavour. If possible, make this at least an hour before
you want to use it. Use a slotted spoon to serve, as you don't want to spoon lots
of vinegar onto each plate!

ASPARAGUS, GOATS' CHEESE & CHERRY TOMATO TART

SERVES 4

These tarts are easy to make, but look very impressive. Cook at the last minute before serving. They are great to eat on a picnic or in the garden. They also would make nice canapés if you make the tarts finger size.

500g / 18 oz packet of puff pastry cut into 4
> (to make starters) or 8-10 (to make canapés)

275g / 10 oz asparagus heads,
> trimmed & cooked in simmering water for 2 minutes

200g / 7 oz St Tola Goats' Cheese, or other soft, mild goats' cheese

8 cherry tomatoes, cut in half

olive oil

sea salt & pepper, to season

parmesan shavings, to taste

METHOD

Heat the oven to 200° C / 400° F / gas 6.

Lightly dust a baking tray with flour. Lay out the four cut-out squares of puff pastry and score a rectangle onto the pastry with a knife, about 2cm in from the edges. Dot the goats' cheese over the puff pastry, within the 2cm / 3/4" border. Place the cherry tomatoes in each corner and lay a quarter of the asparagus on top of each tart. Place on the baking tray, drizzle with olive oil and bake for 20 to 25 minutes until crisp and golden.

Sprinkle with parmesan shavings and serve warm with a nice, mixed-leaf salad.

MAIN COURSES

BALSAMIC & TOMATO ROAST CHICKEN

SERVES 4

This is one of my all-time favourites. It's posh enough to serve at an impromptu dinner party, and it can be put together in the morning and then popped in the oven 30 to 35 minutes before you are going to serve it.

4 thick slices aubergine (eggplant) cut lengthways

4 chicken breast fillets

1 x 14 oz / 400g can whole, peeled tomatoes, drained & quartered

2 tbsps salted capers, rinsed

2 fl. oz / 55ml balsamic vinegar

1 tbsp olive oil

2 tbsps brown sugar

a handful of whole basil leaves and a pinch of cracked black pepper to garnish

METHOD

Preheat the oven to 200° C / 400° F / gas 6. Place the aubergine in the bottom of a baking dish and top each slice with a chicken fillet.
Combine the tomatoes, capers, balsamic vinegar, oil and sugar and spread over the chicken fillets. Bake for 20 to 25 minutes or until the chicken is cooked through. Sprinkle with the basil leaves and cracked pepper and serve with a rocket salad and some parsley mash (see p. 39).

GRATIN OF SEAFOOD WITH PARMESAN & GARLIC CRUMBLE

SERVES 4

1 1/4 lb / 560g cod fillet

juice of 1 lemon

2 oz / 50g button mushrooms

4 oz / 110g prawns, fresh or frozen

1/2 pint / 275ml milk infused with 2 slices of onion, 6 peppercorns and 1 bay leaf

1 oz / 25g butter

1 oz / 25g plain flour

3 oz / 75g fresh, white breadcrumbs, 1 oz / 25g freshly-grated parmesan & 1 clove of garlic, finely chopped, combined together

METHOD

Preheat the oven to 170° C / 325° F / gas mark 3.

Discard the skin on the cod and cut the fillets into thin strips.

Grease 1 large dish or 4 individual dishes or, alternatively, use scallop shells, which look pretty. Put in the fish and sprinkle with lemon juice. Wipe the mushrooms and cut into slices. Add the mushrooms and the prawns to the fish.

Put the milk into a pan with the onion, bay leaf and peppercorns; bring the mixture slowly up to the boil and remove from the heat. Cover the pan and leave to infuse for about 10 minutes, then strain the milk.

Melt the butter in a pan and blend in the flour, taking care not to burn it, but allowing it to cook for a minute or so. Keeping the pan over a low heat, add the infused milk slowly and whisk together until slightly thickened and perfectly smooth. Bring up to the boil and simmer for 1 to 2 minutes.

Spoon the sauce over the fish and sprinkle with the parmesan, garlic and breadcrumb mixture. Bake for 20 to 25 minutes

This is delicious served with mashed potato (see p. 39).

ROAST STUFFED PORK STEAKS WITH ROAST POTATOES & APPLE SAUCE

SERVES 2-3

This is one of my favourite meals. It does take a little bit of organisation, but it's well worth the effort. Pork fillets (steaks) are extremely good value and once cleaned are very lean.

8 oz / 225g white breadcrumbs

1 large pork steak

1 medium onion

2 oz / 50g raisins or sultanas

a good tbsp of parsley, thyme & chives

sea salt & freshly-ground pepper

6-8 oz / 175-225g butter or Stork margarine, melted

6 potatoes, washed and peeled

rosemary, to garnish

METHOD

Pre-heat oven to 190° C / 375° F /gas mark 5.

Clean pork fillet well and remove gristle along the back, as it will cause the fillet to roll up during cooking, and it is also tough. Trim any excess fat or sinew away also. Make a slit in the pork fillet from one end to the other taking care not to cut right through the meat. Flatten it out and make further little cuts in the fillet until it is quite flat.

To make the stuffing, Put the breadcrumbs into a large bowl. Melt the butter or margarine gently. Chop the onion very finely and add to the crumbs along with the raisins, herbs, seasoning and melted fat. Stir well together. You should have a soft, moist stuffing that's not too wet.

Place the stuffing along the flattened pork fillet and roll up the fillet and secure with string. Place in a roasting tin and cover with buttered paper or tinfoil. Add some olive oil to the pan, place the potatoes around the meat and roast in the oven for about 45 to 60 minutes. After the first 20 minutes you can take off the paper and return the pan to the oven to get nice and brown. When cooked, allow to rest for about 10 minutes before cutting the string away. Allow to rest for 10 to 15 minutes before slicing very carefully and serving with apple sauce.

FOR THE APPLE SAUCE

1 lb 5 oz / 600g brambley cooking apples, unpeeled

6 tsps of water

2 tbsps of granulated sugar

METHOD

Peel, quarter and core the apples and slice thinly into a stainless steel saucepan about 8" / 20cm in diameter. Cover with the water and the sugar and slowly bring to the boil. After 1 or 2 minutes lower the heat and stir the apples to make sure that they are all submerged in the water. The sugar will also help to make more juice. Once the apple has broken down (it should take about a minute) stir well, taste for sweetness and put into a nice bowl or sauceboat and serve warm with the roast stuffed pork.

VEGETABLE CHILLI BOWL

*This is a great dish for the whole family; it's low in fat and low GI also.
It's quick to make — you could rustle it up in less than twenty minutes providing
you have all the basics. It's packed with vitamins, so be careful not to overcook the
vegetables — remember, less is more!*

SERVES 4

2 cloves of garlic

2 red chillies, finely chopped

olive oil

2 tsps ground cumin

9 oz / 255g chestnut mushrooms, quartered

14 oz / 400g tin chopped tomatoes

14 oz / 400g tin kidney beans

7 fl. oz / 200ml water or vegetable stock

5 oz / 150g green beans, cut

half-fat crème fraiche to serve

handful of chopped coriander

parmesan cheese, grated (optional)

METHOD

Fry the garlic and chillies in 1 tablespoon of olive oil for 2 minutes.
Add the cumin and mushrooms and cook for 3 minutes. Add the
tomatoes, kidney beans and 200ml water or stock and stir. Simmer for
10 minutes. Add the green beans and cook for another 5 minutes
until the sauce is thickened and the vegetables are tender.
Serve in bowls with some crème fraiche, some grated parmesan,
chopped coriander and nice crusty bread.

THAI CHICKEN & COCONUT CURRY

SERVES 4

This is a very quick curry to make. The amount of red curry paste suggested makes quite a hot curry, so reduce it by half a teaspoon if you prefer a milder curry.

1-2 tbsps Thai red curry paste

1 lb / 400g skinless, boneless chicken fillets, cut into bite-sized pieces

8 oz / 225g broccoli florets

7 fl. oz / 200ml coconut cream

good handful fresh coriander

Thai, jasmine or long-grain rice to serve

METHOD

Blend the curry paste in a small bowl with 2 tablespoons of water, then pour into a pan. Add the chicken with some seasoning and 150ml water. Bring to the boil. Lower the heat, cover the pan tightly and cook for 12 to 15 minutes until just tender.

Meanwhile cook the broccoli in boiling, salted water for 5 minutes Keeping it *al dente*. Drain and cool under cold running water.

Stir into the chicken with the coconut cream. Bring to a gentle simmer and cook for 2 to 3 minutes.

Roughly chop the coriander, keeping some for garnish and stir the rest into the curry. Check the seasoning, garnish with the leftover coriander and serve with rice.

ROAST FILLET OF SALMON WITH ASPARAGUS & SUNDRIED TOMATO PESTO

SERVES 4

This is a healthy meal option, tastes delicious and would be a lovely dish to have when entertaining friends.

2 fillets of salmon portioned into approx. 8 oz / 225g each, with skin

2 bunches of asparagus, blanched

1-2 tbsps olive oil

sea salt & freshly-ground pepper, to season

SUNDRIED TOMATO PESTO

7 oz / 200g sundried tomatoes

8 tbsps lemon juice

2 good handfuls of fresh basil

4 cloves of garlic finely chopped

12-14 fl. oz / 375-400ml extra virgin olive oil

freshly-ground black pepper & sea salt

METHOD

Pre-heat the oven to 200°C / 400°F / gas mark 6. Place the 4 fillets of salmon in a roasting tin. Season with a little freshly ground black pepper and sea salt and drizzle over a tablespoon of olive oil. Roast in the hot oven for approximately 10 minutes. Meanwhile make the tomato pesto by putting all the ingredients into a blender or food processor and blending for 2 to 3 minutes. If the mixture seems to be too thick, add a little extra virgin olive oil and stir to combine. Break the woody ends off the asparagus (about 5 centimetres) and

shortly before serving cook the asparagus in boiling salted water for 6 to 10 minutes, depending on the thickness of the spears. You want the asparagus to still have a 'bite' to it and not be soft. Remove the asparagus from the water and drain. Divide the asparagus spears between four warmed plates, place the hot fillet of salmon on top, skin side up, and put a dessertspoonful of the sun-dried pesto on top of the salmon and serve immediately.

OLD-FASHIONED CORONATION CHICKEN SALAD

SERVES 6

This dish is very easy and is a nice addition to serve as part of a spring buffet.

4 lb / 1.8 kg chicken fillets, cooked

2 bananas, sliced

FOR THE DRESSING

I cup mayonnaise

2 tbsps lemon juice

2 tbsps cream

5 tbsps natural yogurt

I tsp tomato purée

I dessertspoon curry paste or powder (you decide how strong you like it)

2 tbsps mango chutney

sea salt & freshly-ground pepper, to season

I tsp paprika, to dust

METHOD

Dice the chicken fillets into small cubes. Put all the ingredients for the dressing into a bowl and whisk gently until smooth. Then fold the chicken and banana pieces into the mayonnaise, check the seasoning and turn out onto a nice large serving dish and dust with paprika.

LAMB CUTLETS WITH THYME SAUVIGNON SAUCE

SERVES 2

This is a lovely dish for two people to share as it can be made very quickly and it tastes delicious.

1 rack of lamb with 6 to 8 cutlets, trimmed

2 tbsps of fresh thyme off the stalk

2 tbsps of fresh mint, finely chopped

1 tbsp of parsley, finely chopped (optional)

ground black pepper

5 tbsps of Sauvignon Blanc white wine

8 fl. oz / 225ml cream

olive oil

garlic mash (see p. 39) and green beans, to serve

METHOD

Divide the rack into individual cutlets using a sharp knife to carefully cut between the bones. Coat the cutlets in a mixture of 2 tablespoons of fresh thyme and fresh mint finely chopped together; you can also add a little chopped parsley and some ground pepper. Heat 1 tablespoon of olive oil in a large, non-stick frying pan and cook the cutlets over a medium heat for 3 to 4 minutes on each side or until done to your liking. Remove from the pan and keep warm. Return the pan to the heat and add 4 or 5 tablespoons of Sauvignon Blanc white wine and scrape the pan with a wooden spoon to get up all the nice crusty bits of the herbs. Reduce wine by about half, then stir in 5 tablespoons of cream. Simmer for a few seconds stirring to incorporate any pan juices. Season to taste with sea salt and ground black pepper. Pour over the cutlets and serve with garlic mash and green beans, or with a green salad.

If you are not going to serve this dish immediately I would keep the cutlets warm and the sauce separate. You will probably have to add a little extra cream or milk if you prefer and heat through just before you serve the meal. I would plate the cutlets first and drizzle the sauce over them. If you have any left over, serve it in a little dish.

DESSERTS

•••••••••••••••••••• CHAMPAGNE SYLLABUB

SERVES 4-6

YOU NEED 4-6 NICE SUNDAE
GLASSES, OR NICE WINE
GLASSES

This is a very pretty and simple dessert and it has a wonderful smoothness. It looks very special served in beautiful glasses

1/2 pint / 275ml cream

4 tbsps icing sugar

7 fl. oz / 200ml good champagne

Amaretti Biscuits, crushed, or blueberries

little macaroons (optional), to serve

METHOD

Whip the cream and sugar together to soft peaks then whip in the champagne until you have a soft, spoonable mixture. Half fill the glasses with the syllabub then add a layer of the crushed amaretti or blueberries and cover with the remaining syllabub. Decorate with a little more crushed amaretti.

Chill in the fridge for a couple of hours.

Serve with blueberries and a macaroon on the side.

SERIOUS SHERRY TRIFLE

SERVES 8–10

2 packs trifle sponges, or 16 sponge fingers

1 tin (11 oz / 310g) mandarin oranges, drained (keep the juice)

1–2 tbsps caster sugar

1 jar (13 oz / 370g) good quality raspberry jam

4 tbsps Harvey's Bristol Cream sherry

1 pint / 570ml custard (to make fresh, see opposite page)

1 pint / 570ml cream, lightly whipped

mint leaves, redcurrants or grated chocolate, to garnish

METHOD

Split the sponge fingers in half and spread generously with jam. Overlap the sponge fingers in a nice bowl together with the mandarin oranges. Put the drained juice from the oranges into a small saucepan with the caster sugar and dissolve over a gentle heat. When the sugar has dissolved, add the sherry, bring up to the boil and then let simmer for about 5 minutes. Cool and then drizzle over the sponge fingers, making sure to coat as much of the sponge as possible. Next, cover the whole lot with the custard, cool again and then decorate by covering the surface with softly whipped cream and garnishing with mint leaves, grated chocolate or redcurrants.

FRESH CUSTARD OR · · · · · · · · · · · · ·
CRÈME ANGLAISE

SERVES 8

This basic sauce is usually flavoured with vanilla, but can be made with any number of other flavourings, such as lemon or orange rind or mint.

1 pint / 570ml full-fat milk

1 vanilla pod or other flavouring

3 egg yolks

1 oz /25g caster sugar

METHOD

Add the vanilla pod (if you are using one) to the milk and bring the milk almost to the boil. Beat the egg yolks with the sugar until thick and light. Whisk in half the hot milk and then whisk the mixture back into the remaining milk. Cook over a very low heat, stirring constantly with a wooden spoon until the custard thickens slightly. Your finger should leave a clear trail when drawn across the back of the spoon. Remove from the heat at once and strain. Cool, cover tightly and chill.

The custard can be kept for up to two days in the refrigerator.

PASSION FRUIT ROULADE

SERVES 10

6 large free-range eggs

4 oz / 110g caster sugar

2 lemons

2 heaped tbsps plain flour

icing sugar for dusting

FOR THE FILLING

12 oz / 350g lemon or orange curd, good quality

9-10 fl. oz / 280-300ml cream

8 passion fruits, ripe and wrinkled

caster sugar, to finish

METHOD

Preheat the oven to 200° C / 400° F / gas mark 6.

Line a 36 x 30 cm baking tray with a piece of baking parchment, making sure that it comes up the sides.

Separate the eggs, putting the yolks into a food mixer and the whites into a bowl large enough to beat them in. Add the sugar to the yolks and whisk until thick, pale and creamy.

Grate the zest from both the lemons, taking care not to include the bitter white pith underneath, squeeze the juice of one of them and set aside.

Beat the egg whites until they are stiff and capable of standing in a soft peak, and set them aside. Then fold the juice and the zest into the egg-yolk and sugar mixture followed by the sifted flour and then the beaten egg whites. Add the egg whites slowly and firmly, but gently, so that the air is not knocked out of them as you mix them in. It is crucial not to over-mix. Scoop the mixture into the lined baking tin, smoothing it gently out to the edges.

Bake for about 10 minutes until the top is very lightly coloured and it feels softly set. Let it cool for a few minutes.

Put a piece of greaseproof paper on a work surface and cover lightly with caster sugar, then turn the roulade out onto it. The cake should be crust side down. Carefully peel away the paper and cover the roulade with a clean, moist tea towel. This will hold even overnight.

When you are ready to roll the cake, remove the towel and spread the lemon or orange curd over the surface, then whip the cream until it will stand in soft peaks and spread it over the curd. Cut the passion fruits in half and spread the juice and seeds over the cream.

Now roll up the roulade, either from the short end for a fuller roulade, or from the long side to give you a longer thinner roulade. Dust with icing sugar and serve!

ALMOND ICE CREAM

SERVES 10

This has to be one of my favourite ice creams. The ingredients are so simple and the taste is superb; the praline gives it that 'rich' flavour. It's really easy to make and you don't need an ice cream machine!! It looks very impressive for a dinner party and can be frozen in a terrine tin lined with cling film, or in a bowl if you prefer, and then turned out onto a long white rectangular plate decorated with redcurrants and mint. This ice cream melts very quickly, so don't remove it from the freezer until you are ready to serve dessert.

PRALINE

2 oz / 50g caster sugar

2 tbsps water

2 oz / 50g unblanched almonds

ICE-CREAM

4 eggs, separated

4 ozs / 110g icing sugar, sifted

1/2 pint / 300ml cream, lightly whipped

redcurrants and mint, for decoration

METHOD

Put the caster sugar and water in a pan. Heat slowly until the sugar has dissolved then add the almonds. Cook quickly, moving frequently – do not stir – until the mixture is a deep, golden brown.

Turn out onto an oiled baking tray. Leave until set, then pulverize in the food processor or put between a double layer of greaseproof paper and crush with a rolling pin.

Meanwhile, whisk the egg yolks until blended. In another bowl whisk the whites until stiff then whisk in the icing sugar a teaspoon at a time, as if making a meringue. Whisk the egg yolks into the meringue mixture with the cream. Turn into a 2 pint plastic container and cover; freeze for two hours. Then turn the mixture into a large bowl, whisk until smooth, and stir in the praline. Return to the freezer in the covered container and freeze until required.

Delicious, naturally, and so easy to make!

CHERRY & ALMOND EASTER CAKE, OR MOTHER'S DAY CAKE

SERVES 10–12

This will cut into approximately twelve slices and is really simple to make. It's what I call 'almost all-in-one cake'. Everyone loves it, and it cuts beautifully. It also keeps for at least a week as the grated marzipan helps to keep it moist. Decorate according to the occasion!

9 oz / 225g butter, softened, plus a little extra for greasing

6 oz / 175g golden caster sugar

5 eggs, beaten

9 oz / 255g self-raising flour, plus an extra 2 tablespoons

1 tsp baking powder

zest of 1 orange, plus the juice

9 oz / 255g natural marzipan, coarsely grated (it's easier to grate if you chill it beforehand)

7 oz / 200g glacé cherries, halved

FOR THE DECORATION

4 oz / 110g icing sugar sifted

2 oz / 50g toasted flaked almonds

12 natural whole glacé cherries

zest of 1 orange (optional)

METHOD

Heat the oven to 170° C / 325° F / gas 3 and butter and line a 8" / 20cm round, loose-bottomed, deep, cake tin. Beat the butter and sugar together until light and fluffy. Add the beaten eggs, the flour, baking powder, orange zest and juice and beat well until thick, creamy and evenly mixed. Toss the cherries in the extra 2 tablespoons of flour, to stop them sinking to the bottom of the cake while cooking, and fold into the batter along with the marzipan. Take care to mix the grated marzipan well into the batter. Spoon into the prepared tin, level and bake for 1 hour and 30 minutes or until well-risen and golden. A skewer will come out clean when ready. Leave to cool in the tin for 10 minutes then turn onto a cooling rack to cool completely. Mix the sieved icing sugar with 1 tablespoon of hot water to make a loose, but not-too-runny icing. Scatter the almonds over the top of the cake and position the 12 glacé cherries (to represent the 12 apostles) around the edge, using a dot of icing to fix. Drizzle the icing over the cake and finish with a scattering of orange zest.

TO MAKE CUPCAKES:

Use the cherry and almond cake mixture and divide between 24
bun cases. Bake at 180° C / 350° F / gas 4 for 20 to 25 minutes until well risen and golden. Cover with the glacé icing and top with mini chocolate eggs.
Great for Easter!

SUMMER

STARTERS

DELICIOUS PEA & MINT SOUP

SERVES 4

This soup is lovely and light, yet quite filling. It uses no flour, which is another bonus, and can be served hot or cold. If serving cold I would sprinkle the top with chive flowers, which would look lovely against the vibrant green!

1 1/2 pints / 900ml homemade chicken or vegetable stock

2 oz / 50g butter

5 oz / 150g finely-chopped onion

1 garlic clove finely-chopped (optional)

1 lb / 450g frozen peas

2 tbsps finely-chopped, fresh garden mint

sea salt & freshly-ground white pepper

a little softly-whipped cream to swirl on the top of soup

some mint sprigs or chopped mint, to garnish

METHOD

Heat the stock. In another pan, melt the butter on a low heat, add the onion and garlic and season with salt and pepper and sweat for 3 to 4 minutes. Add the peas and cover with the stock. Bring to the boil and simmer for 6 to 10 minutes with the lid off. Add the chopped mint, remove from the heat and liquidise until smooth. Check the seasoning and serve with a swirl of cream and chopped mint on top. You may find that you need to add another drop of water to the soup if you feel it is a little thick.

PRAWN & MELON COCKTAIL

SERVES 4

For the more adventurous of you, whisk a teaspoon of curry paste into the mayonnaise!

7 oz / 200g shelled prawns, defrosted if frozen, drained & dried

1 1/2 lb / 700g green or orange melon flesh cut into small cubes

(if desired, 9 oz / 255g of the melon could be ready-prepared melon

balls to vary the shapes)

half a head of crisp lettuce leaves (e.g iceberg)

1/4 tsp chilli flakes

4 fl. oz / 125 ml mayonnaise

smoked paprika for dusting (or normal paprika if smoked is

unavailable)

METHOD

Mix the prawns and the melon and leave to drain in a small sieve set over a bowl.
You could do this the day before.

Discard the liquid that has collected in the bowl.

Mix the chilli flakes into the mayonnaise then fold into the prawns and melon
and season lightly. Arrange the lettuce leaves on plates or alternatively shred the
lettuce leaves and put into nice cocktail glasses or sundae glasses, pile the prawn
and melon cocktail on top, dust with smoked paprika and serve.

PAN-FRIED MACKEREL WITH HERB BUTTER AND TOAST

SERVES 4

This is one of my all time favourites, especially cooked straight from the sea.

4 whole mackerel, cleaned and filleted

2 oz / 50g flour, seasoned with salt and pepper

2 oz / 50g butter

approx 8 slices of bread, for toasting

FOR THE HERB BUTTER

4 oz / 110g butter, softened

1 tspb parsley

1 tspb chives

sea salt & black pepper to season

1 tsp lemon zest, optional

METHOD

Make the herb butter first by putting the softened butter in a bowl and adding in all the herbs and seasoning, and the lemon zest if you are using it, and mixing well together. Spoon the butter mixture out onto a square of baking parchment and, folding over the parchment, make a long roll of the butter. Twist the ends of the parchment and place in the freezer or fridge to harden until you are ready to use it. Add the remaining butter to the frying pan and heat, dip the mackerel fillets in the seasoned flour, taking care to shake off the excess flour, and place meaty side down in the foaming butter. Allow to cook for 4 to 5 minutes before turning over to cook on the skin side for the same amount of time. Keep warm in the oven while cooking the remaining fillets. Serve on warm plates garnished with two circles of herby butter and a lemon quarter. Make sure to have plenty of hot, buttered toast to go with the fish!

SIMPLE SUMMER SALAD

SERVES 4

For the mixed salad in this recipe, I like to use a nice mixture or 'mesclun' of salad leaves such as rocket, lamb's lettuce, parsley, basil leaves, red chicory, oak leaf, nasturtiums and so on.

1 tbsp Dijon mustard

1 tbsp red wine vinegar

a pinch of sea salt

2 large eggs, at room temperature

3 tbsps extra virgin olive oil

2 cups croutons (bread cubes cut into small cubes)

8 cups mixed salad leaves torn into pieces

2 tomatoes cored and diced

2 fat cloves of garlic, finely chopped or minced

METHOD

Place the mustard in a small bowl. Whisk in the vinegar and salt to taste; mix well. Slowly pour in the extra virgin olive oil and whisk until the mixture is slightly blended. Put to one side. Place the eggs in a saucepan and cook uncovered until the bubbles rise to the top of the pan. Reduce the heat and simmer for 8 minutes. Pour off the water and stop the cooking by running under the cold tap for a few minutes. When the eggs are cool, crack, peel and coarsely chop them, and set them aside. Heat the 3 tablespoons of oil in a pan over a medium heat. When the oil is hot, but not smoking, add the bread cubes and toss to coat entirely in oil. Sauté until the bread is browned on all sides, which should take about 3 to 4 minutes. Set aside. Place the salad leaves in a large, shallow, salad bowl. Sprinkle on the tomatoes, eggs, garlic and croutons. Just before serving, add the dressing and toss gently but thoroughly until the greens are evenly coated and serve.

MAIN COURSES

ROSEMARY ROAST LEG OF LAMB

SERVES 6-8

6-7 lb / 3kg leg of lamb, from your butcher

some fresh sprigs of rosemary

2 cloves of garlic

2-3 tbsps of olive oil

sea salt & freshly-ground black pepper

12-16 medium sized potatoes, peeled, washed & dried

1/4 pint / 150ml lamb or chicken stock

2-3 tbsp white wine

METHOD

Pre-heat the oven to 200° C / 400° F / gas 6. Put the rosemary sprigs on the bottom of the roasting tin and place the lamb on top of the herbs. Cut the two cloves of garlic into small slivers and, making little incisions all over the top of the lamb, insert the slivers of garlic. Drizzle over the olive oil, and sprinkle with the sea salt and the freshly-ground pepper. Place the roasting tin in the preheated oven and roast the lamb for twenty-five minutes. When this time is up add the potatoes to the tin, drizzle a further tablespoon of olive oil over them, and return to the oven. Reduce the oven temperature to 180° C / 350° F /gas 4 and cook for a further hour. Check once or twice during that time as the potatoes will need turning over during cooking to ensure they are nicely browned on all sides. If you like your lamb well done, leave the meat in the oven for a further 15 to 20 minutes, but remove the potatoes to a serving dish and keep warm. When the lamb is cooked remove it from the roasting tin, place it on a large serving dish and keep warm. To make the gravy, tilt the roasting tin and pour off the excess oil or remove with a tablespoon. Put the tin back on a medium heat and deglaze the tin with 2 or 3 tablespoons of white wine (optional). Add 1/4 pint of lamb or chicken stock and bring up to the boil scraping the tin to get up all the nice meaty bits. Season with salt and pepper and put into a sauce boat to serve at the table with the lamb, roast potatoes and some mint sauce.

FILLET OF BEEF WITH RED WINE & MUSTARD CREAM JUS

SERVES 4

1 lb 12 oz / 800g approx fillet of beef, trimmed

2 tbsps olive oil

ground black pepper

small wine glass of red wine

8 fl. oz / 250ml beef stock

2 dessertspoons of grainy mustard

10 fl. oz / 300ml cream

1 tsp thyme leaves

sea salt & ground black pepper

METHOD

Pre-heat the oven to 200° C /400° F / gas 6.

Put the olive oil in a roasting tin and heat on top of the hob.

When the oil starts to smoke, put in the fillet of beef. Grind some black pepper over the beef and place the roasting tin in the preheated oven. Roast for 30 to 35 minutes if you like your beef rare. Remove the beef to a serving dish and keep warm. Meanwhile, remove the oil from the tin with a tablespoon and return the tin to the hob. Allow it to get warm and add the red wine, scraping the tin to unstick all the nice meaty bits on the bottom of the tin, add the beef stock and the mustard and thyme leaves and bring up to the boil, stir well to blend the juices and add the cream slowly and incorporate into the sauce. Season with sea salt and freshly ground black pepper. Slice the beef thinly and place on a nice serving dish, drizzle the sauce over the meat or serve separately in a jug.

BLACKENED CHICKEN WITH SWEETCORN SALSA

SERVES 8

8 large skinless chicken fillets (about 7 ozs each)

2 tbsp extra virgin olive oil

SPICES

2 tsps salt

2 tsps dried oregano

2 tsps dried thyme

I tsp black pepper

I tsp white pepper

I tsp onion powder

I tsp garlic salt/powder

I tsp paprika

I tsp cayenne

FOR THE SALSA

I lb / 450g sweetcorn

3-4 tomatoes, diced

I whole cucumber, cut in I/2 lengthways and I/2 again to give 4 quarters, remove the seeds and dice

I large red onion, peeled and diced

2 tbsps coriander & flat-leaf parsley

6 tbsps extra virgin oil

juice of I lime

2-3 drops of Tabasco (optional)

sea salt & freshly-ground black pepper

METHOD

Pre-heat the oven to 200° C /400° F / gas 6.

In a large bowl, mix together all the blackening spices.

Make three or four slits, not all the way through, in the chicken fillets and sprinkle the spices on both sides of the chicken, or on one side only if you don't like too much heat!! Heat a large frying pan over a high heat and add the oil. Add the chicken fillets three at a time, and fry quite fast so that you sear and roast the spices very well. Don't be tempted to add too many fillets to the pan at once or you will lower the temperature and the fillets will 'sweat'. When each fillet is well seared place in a roasting tray and bake in the preheated oven for about 10 to 15 minutes. Serve the chicken either hot or cold with sweetcorn salsa. Tiny rosemary roasties (see p. 37) go very well with this dish.

TO MAKE THE SWEETCORN SALSA

Cook the sweetcorn according to the instructions on the packet. Drain and cool under running water, drain again. Meanwhile dice the tomatoes, cucumber and red onion and add to the salsa. Blend the olive oil, lime juice and Tabasco and pour over the salsa. Chop the coriander and parsley and add to the salad.

Season well with sea salt and freshly ground black pepper. Cover with clingfilm and place in the fridge until ready to serve. This can be made a couple of hours in advance. It goes very well with the blackened chicken, or as a salad on its own, and has a lovely clean taste.

ROAST COD ON SPICY PUY LENTILS

SERVES 4

2 tbsps olive oil, plus extra for greasing

2 tsps mild curry powder

4 x 7 oz / 200g pieces thick cod fillet

FOR THE SPICY PUY LENTILS

10 oz / 275g puy lentils

1 tbsp olive oil

2 fat cloves of garlic, finely chopped

1 medium red chilli, de-seeded and finely chopped

1/2 tsp ground cumin

1 small red onion, finely chopped

4 tbsps fresh chicken stock

lemon juice, to taste

3 tbsps chopped, fresh coriander

1 small tub of low-fat natural yogurt

cayenne pepper and fresh coriander sprigs, to garnish

METHOD

Pre-heat the oven to 220° C / 425° F / gas 7.

Cook the lentils in a pan of simmering water for 20 minutes or until tender. After 15 minutes mix the olive oil for the fish with the curry powder. Brush all over the cod and season. Heat an ovenproof frying pan over a medium-high heat. Grease with a little oil and add the cod, meaty side down. Fry for 2 minutes until light golden, turn over and transfer the pan to the oven. Roast for 5 minutes. Drain the lentils. Heat the oil in a clean pan, add the garlic, chilli and cumin. Once the oil is sizzling, stir in the lentils, onion and stock and warm through. Add lemon juice and seasoning to taste. Stir in the coriander. Spoon onto warm plates and place the cod on top. Serve with the yogurt and coriander.

MARINATED FILLET OF PORK

SERVES 3-4

1 1/2-2 lb / 700-900g pork fillet

2 oz / 60g butter

1 large onion, chopped

8 fl. oz / 250ml chicken stock

3 tomatoes, skinned and sliced

a handful of parsley or coriander, chopped

sea salt & freshly-ground black pepper

FOR THE MARINADE

2 tbsp soy sauce

1 tbsp Worcestershire sauce

4 tbsp tomato ketchup

1 tbsp bottled fruit sauce (available in supermarkets, e.g. HP Fruity)

1 tbsp honey

1 teaspoon French mustard

METHOD

Cut the pork fillet into bite-sized chunks. Melt one third of the butter in a flameproof dish; add the sauces and seasonings for the marinade and mix together. Put in the pork pieces and turn them around so that they are well coated. Leave them to marinate for 20 minutes or longer. Heat a sauté pan, drop in the rest of the butter and, while it is still foaming, remove the strips of pork from the marinade, drain and add to the pan. Add the onion and sauté slowly with the pork until coloured. Pour in the stock, cover the pan and simmer for 25 to 30 minutes. Lift out the pork, dish up on a hot serving dish and add the marinade to the pan. Reduce it until sticky, then add the sliced tomatoes; cook them for 3 to 4 minutes then spoon the sauce over the meat. Sprinkle with chopped parsley or coriander and serve with rice and a green salad.

CHICKEN SALAD WITH PALE GREEN FRUIT

SERVES 6–8

This cold salad makes a lovely light main course to serve on a warm day. If you don't like tarragon you could use parsley instead, and you can substitute white wine vinegar for the tarragon vinegar if you prefer.

6 large, boneless, skinless chicken fillets

8 fl. oz / 225ml whipping cream

12 oz / 350g honeydew melon balls

12 oz / 350g cucumber balls (avoid the seeds)

5 oz / 150g green, seedless grapes

4 oz / 110g blanched, sliced almonds

1 tsp freshly-ground black pepper

1 tsp salt

grated zest of 1 lemon

2 oz / 50g chopped fresh dill

FOR THE LEMON MAYONNAISE

10 oz / 275g good quality mayonnaise

2 tbsps tarragon vinegar

2 tbsps fresh lemon juice

2 tbsps Dijon-style mustard

8 fl. oz / 250ml mild olive oil

8 fl. oz / 250ml corn oil

1 bunch of fresh tarragon, leaves chopped

a little ground white pepper

1 teaspoon sea salt

grated zest of a lemon

METHOD

Pre-heat oven to 180° C / 350° F / gas 4.

Arrange the chicken breasts in a single layer in a large baking pan. Spread evenly with the cream and bake for 20 to 25 minutes. Cool completely, then remove the chicken from the cream and discard the juices. While the chicken is cooling, prepare the lemon mayonnaise; place the mayonnaise, vinegar, lemon juice and mustard in a bowl and slowly whisk in the oils in a steady stream. Gently fold in the tarragon leaves, sea salt, pepper and lemon zest.

Cut the chicken into dice-sized pieces and place in a large bowl. Add the melon and the cucumber balls, and the grapes and almonds, and toss to combine.

Sprinkle with the pepper, salt, lemon zest and all but 2 tablespoons of the dill and toss again until thoroughly mixed.

Fold in the mayonnaise. Spoon onto a nice serving platter and garnish with the remaining dill.

DESSERTS

ITALIAN FRUIT SALAD

SERVES 4-6

*This dessert is really so easy and can be made in minutes.
You know summer has arrived when you have all this delicious
fruit at home — it's also very good for you and not fattening!*

4 oz / 110g raspberries

4 oz / 110g strawberries, small ones or fraises du bois, or sliced

4 oz / 110g blueberries

4 oz / 110g blackberries

1 or 2 peaches

juice of 1/2 lemon

barely 2 oz / 50g sugar

dessertspoonful fresh mint, finely chopped

miniature shortbread biscuits, to serve (optional)

METHOD

Combine all the berries and the sliced peaches in a nice bowl and sprinkle with
the sugar and fresh lemon juice. Fold in the finely chopped mint and stir. Taste
and add more sugar or juice if you wish. This salad should not be dressed until
just before you are going to serve it. It can be served with crème fraiche, vanilla
ice-cream, softly whipped cream and tiny shortbread biscuits, or both.

LINZER TORTE

SERVES 8–10

8 oz / 225g plain flour

4 oz / 110g butter

4 oz / 110g caster sugar

1 whole egg

1 egg yolk

2 oz / 50g almonds, ground, without blanching, in food processor

pinch of salt

a big pinch of ground cinnamon

grated lemon rind to flavour, about 1/2 a lemon

1 lb / 450g fresh raspberries brought to the boil and cooked rapidly

for 2-3 minutes with sugar to sweeten and allowed to cool

METHOD

Pre-heat the oven to 180° C /350° F /gas mark 4.

Sift the flour with a pinch of salt and the cinnamon and make a 'well' in the centre. Place the butter, sugar, whole egg and yolk, and the lemon rind in this well and sprinkle the ground almonds on the flour. Work the ingredients together with the fingertips of one hand – hold the other one behind your back. This helps to prevent you overworking the pastry and keeps one hand clean! When the pastry has come together, wrap in parchment paper and leave to rest in a cool place for at least half hour.

Roll out the pastry to between 1/4" and 1/2" (5mm and 1cm) thick and line into a 9" / 23cm flan ring or dish, leaving enough to cut into strips to make a lattice. Fill with the cold raspberry mixture and put the lattice of the pastry across the top. Bake in a moderate oven for 20 to 30 minutes. Allow to cool and then brush with a redcurrant glaze.

RICH CHOCOLATE MOUSSE

SERVES 6-8,
AS CHOCOLATE POTS

This is a rich mousse, but it is really very good. Men love it and it is not too much of a sweet fix after a great dinner!! This dessert needs to be made the day before you intend to serve it, as the mousse needs to be refrigerated overnight. This dish contains raw egg, so do not serve to the very old or very young.

6 oz / 175g good quality chocolate

2 1/2 fl. oz / 75ml water

1/2 oz / 15g butter

1-2 tbsps rum or brandy, or 1 tsp vanilla extract

3 organic or free-range eggs, separated

chocolate shavings, to sprinkle

1/4 pint / 5 fl. oz cream, whipped, to serve

METHOD

Break up the chocolate and put the chocolate and water in a stainless steel saucepan over a low heat and let melt to a thick cream. Take off the heat and allow the mixture to cool for a minute or two, then add the butter and the yolks of the eggs, one by one, beating well between each addition. Add the rum or vanilla extract to taste. Whisk the whites stiffly and fold gently but briskly into the chocolate. When mixed, pour into small pots and leave in the fridge overnight.

Just before serving the following day put a tiny blob of whipped cream on the top of the chocolate and maybe some chocolate shavings.

CARAMEL ORANGE SALAD

SERVES 4-6

This salad is low in fat, super healthy and counts as one of the 5-a-day. It's also a good source of vitamin C. It goes with everything from a few scoops of ice-cream to a luscious dark chocolate cake.

5 nice juicy oranges

6 oz / 175g caster sugar

METHOD

Use a peeler to remove strips of zest from three of the oranges and finely slice these into strands. Place the zest in a small pan of cold water and bring to a rolling boil, then drain, run under a cold tap, drain again and set aside. Juice one orange and set aside and carefully use a sharp knife to remove the outer peel of the rest of the oranges then slice them across into wagon-wheeled shaped pieces, about a finger thickness.

Tip the sugar into a frying pan with 4 tablespoons of water; place on a high heat and boil for 3 to 4 minutes until caramelized and golden. Carefully pour about a third of the caramel onto a greased tray and set aside to cool. Place the pan back on the heat. Toss the zest into the pan and cook for a few moments until it becomes shiny and candied. Pour in the orange juice (be careful as it will splutter) and throw in the orange slices. Shake everything together gently then transfer to a nice serving dish. By now the caramel on the baking tray should have cooled and hardened — break it into shards, crumble them over the oranges and serve.

HAZELNUT CAKE

SERVES 8

This is a wonderfully light and nutty cake, which can be served for afternoon tea or as a light dessert. The recipe does not use flour, so it's excellent for people who cannot tolerate flour, like coeliacs; it also has a great flavour, which is sometimes lacking in gluten-free food!!

If you are serving this as a dessert, a raspberry coulis and some fresh raspberries would go very well with this, as would whipped cream and chocolate sauce.

7 oz / 200g unblanched hazelnuts

5 eggs

6 oz / 175g caster sugar

4 oz / 110g butter, melted

1 tsp vanilla extract

METHOD

Heat the oven to 180° C / 350° F / gas 4.

Butter and line the base of an 8" / 20cm round deep cake tin. Grind the hazelnuts in a food processor or blender until they are as fine as you can get them. If they seem damp, spread them out on a baking sheet to dry for half an hour or so, mixing occasionally.

Separate the eggs into two large bowls. Tip the sugar onto the egg yolks and whisk for about 3 to 4 minutes or until the whisk leaves a trail on the surface when the whisk blades are lifted.

Gradually whisk in the melted butter, not too hot, then fold in the hazelnuts and vanilla. Whisk the egg whites until stiff, then fold into cake mixture in four equal batches, being very careful not to knock out all the air.

Pour into the prepared tin and bake for 50 to 60 minutes until the cake feels firm and bounces back when pressed in the centre. Cool in the tin for 10 minutes then turn out. Peel off the paper and cool fully on a wire tray.

STARTERS

GREEN SALAD WITH GOATS' CHEESE AND SUNDRIED TOMATOES

SERVES 6

6-12 sundried tomatoes

4-6 oz / 110-175g French or Irish goats' cheese

a mixture of green lettuces and mixed baby leaves: oak leaf, rocket, watercress, baby spinach

tiny spring onions or scallions cut on the diagonal into 1" / 2cm pieces

FOR THE DRESSING

2 tbsps red wine vinegar or balsamic vinegar

6 tbsps of extra virgin olive oil

1 clove garlic, crushed

1/2 tsp of Meaux mustard or Lakeshore wholegrain honey mustard

sea salt & freshly-ground black pepper

fresh basil leaves

METHOD

Whisk all the dressing ingredients together. Wash and dry the lettuce leaves and tear into small pieces.

Just before serving, toss the lettuces in just enough dressing to make the leaves glisten. Arrange in a nice wide serving dish and crumble in some goats' cheese, scattering it over the leaves along with the sundried tomatoes.

Tear the fresh basil and sprinkle over the top; serve immediately.

CAULIFLOWER SOUP

SERVES 4–6

This is another very quick soup to put together, and is quite filling.
If you find it too thick you can add extra stock or milk to achieve the
consistency you would like. Serve this soup piping hot, but do not allow
it to boil.

2 oz / 50g butter

1 large onion, finely chopped

1 clove garlic, finely chopped

1 medium cauliflower, florets only, no leaves

1 3/4 pint / 1 litre chicken or vegetable stock

4 tbsps milk or cream

croutons or toast, and chopped, fresh parsley, to garnish

METHOD

Heat the butter in a large, heavy pan. Add the onion and garlic and sweat gently
until soft. Add the cauliflower and stock then cover and simmer for an hour.
Purée the soup with a hand blender, or in a food processor, then return it to a
clean pan and check the seasoning. Stir in the milk or cream and re-heat the
soup to simmering point. Scatter the croutons, or the toast cut into cubes, on
top of the soup and sprinkle with parsley before serving.

CHICKEN LIVER PÂTÉ

SERVES 6–8

This chicken liver pâté is absolutely delicious, although strong in flavour. If you like your pâté creamier, just add about 2 or 3 extra ounces of butter. This pâté is great on toast or crostini, as a canapé or as an antipasto starter. It keeps in the fridge for 2 or 3 days, if covered.

5 oz / 150g chicken livers with all membrane and fat removed

1 tbsp olive oil or butter

2 tbsps brandy, port or marsala

1 large clove of garlic, crushed or grated

1 tsp thyme, sage and parsley, or a mixture of all three

3 oz / 75g butter

METHOD

Fry the livers in the olive oil or butter over a low to medium heat until cooked through. While they are cooking, measure the alcohol into a small bowl. When the livers are cooked transfer them to a food processor and whiz together. Put the pan back on the heat – do not wash it first – and add the alcohol, garlic and chopped herbs. Take care here, if the pan is very hot it will flame; it's ok if it does, but you just need to stand back from the heat for a few seconds until the flame subsides. Stir the herbs and garlic around the pan, scraping all the nice, tasty bits from the sides of the pan and then scrape the mixture into the food processor on top of the livers. Whizz together and leave to cool before you add the butter (or else the butter will melt). When the livers have cooled add the butter an ounce at a time while whizzing the pâté until it is smooth. Season to taste.

Spread the pâté out onto some crostini and garnish with a few chives, parsley or tomato concassé. It's also great on toast or French bread.

You could also line a 1 lb / 450g loaf tin or terrine tin with cling film, pour the mixture in and smooth the surface. Cover with the overlapping cling film and refrigerate for a few hours. To serve, slice like a loaf of bread and serve on individual plates with some toast or brown bread.

MINESTRONE SOUP

SERVES 6-8

Healthy, healthy, healthy!

1 large onion

2 medium leeks

2-3 carrots

1 head of celery, outside leaves removed

2 large potatoes, diced evenly

2 plump cloves of garlic, finely chopped

2 oz / 50g butter

1 tbsp tomato purée

2 1/2 pints / 1 1/2 litres water or stock (chicken or vegetable)

2 oz / 50g spaghetti, broken into small pieces

sea salt & ground black pepper, to season

basil oil, pesto or freshly-grated parmesan, to serve

METHOD

Dice all the vegetables, except the potatoes, into small, evenly-sized squares. Put the butter into a saucepan and add the chopped vegetables to 'sweat' until all of them have been glazed. This process will take about 20 minutes. Then add 2 tablespoons of tomato purée and mix well. Cover completely with the water or stock. Allow to come to the boil slowly and continue cooking on a medium heat for about 20 to 25 minutes. Check once or twice that they are not cooking too quickly. While the vegetables are cooking, dice the potatoes into small squares; when the vegetables are almost cooked add the diced potatoes, the broken up spaghetti and the ground, black pepper.

After about 15 minutes, when the potatoes should be tender, but not mushy, the soup is ready to serve. Serve with chopped parsley; a little chopped cooked ham is also very nice added to the soup before serving along with some very good bread and basil oil, pesto (see p. 32) or grated parmesan.

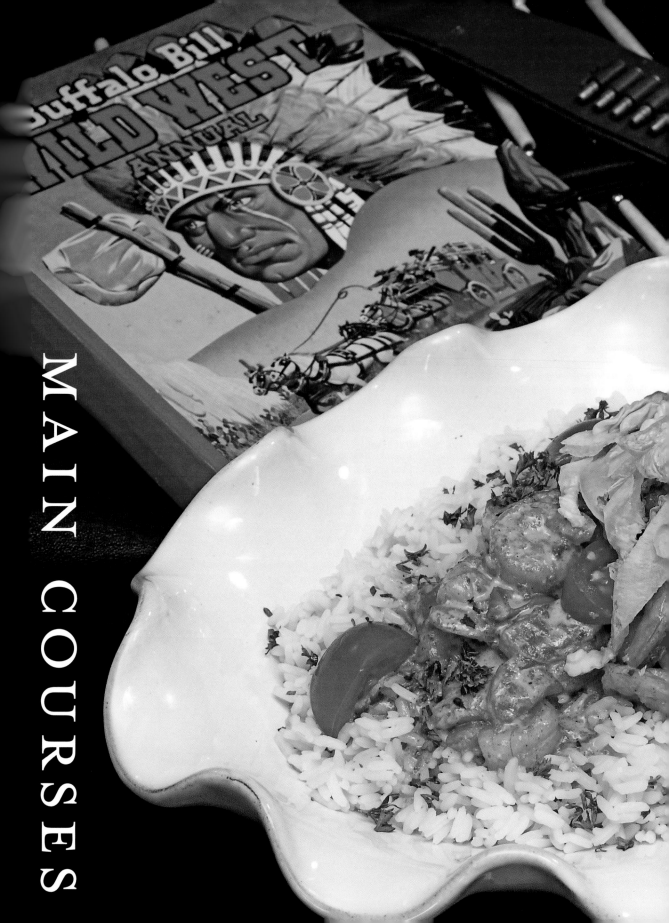

MAIN COURSES

SCAMPI INDIANA

SERVES 2-6

(AS STARTER OR MAIN

COURSE)

This is a very unusual dish, really different and it only takes about 15 minutes to prepare. It's a nice meal for two people or you could serve it as a starter for four to six people. This dish is best served as soon as it is cooked.

1 lb / 400g raw prawns or frozen raw prawns, peeled if possible

3-4 tbsps oil

pinch of salt & pepper

2 fl. oz / 55ml brandy

1 tbsp curry powder

1/2 tsp garlic salt

7 fl.oz / 200ml cream

6-8 tomatoes

a few drops of Tabasco

1 butterhead lettuce

parsley, to garnish

METHOD

Peel the prawns, if not already shelled. Heat the oil and fry the prawns quickly. Season to taste.

Add the brandy, light it with a match and allow it to evaporate. Add the curry and garlic powder and stir in well while frying. Add the cream, and then the tomato segments. Bring to the boil and simmer slowly for 2 to 3 minutes. Add seasoning, spices and Tabasco to taste. Just before serving, add the shredded lettuce, garnish with parsley and serve with rice.

CHICKEN MILANO

SERVES 4

This is a really filling, comforting autumn dish; it's delicious served with baked potatoes and a green salad.

4 chicken fillets

2 oz / 50g seasoned wholemeal flour

2 oz / 50g grated parmesan cheese

I egg beaten

2-3 tbsps of sunflower oil

4 oz / 110g mozzarella cheese sliced

I tbsp olive oil

I finely-chopped onion

I finely-chopped clove of garlic

2 large courgettes diced small

I 14 oz / 400g tin chopped tomatoes

I tbsp tomato purée

I tsp dried basil

I tsp dried oregano

sea salt & freshly-ground black pepper

some nice basil sprigs or leaves and freshly-grated parmesan,

to garnish

METHOD

Heat your oven to 180° C / 350° F / gas 4.

Mix the seasoned flour with 1 oz / 25g of the parmesan cheese and dip each chicken fillet first in the beaten egg and then in the flour mixture coating both sides. Melt the sunflower oil in a frying pan and when it is hot add the chicken fillets, you may have to do two at a time, and fry until they are golden on both sides, transfer them to a rectangular baking dish that is big enough to take the four fillets, and fry the remaining two fillets and transfer to baking dish.

Cover each fillet with slices of mozzarella cheese.

Wipe the frying pan clean with kitchen paper and add the olive oil to it and heat until it is hot. Add the chopped onion and garlic and cook over a gentle heat for 5 minutes. Add the courgettes and cook these for 2 to 3 minutes and then add the tomatoes, tomato purée, basil, oregano, salt and pepper. Let the sauce

simmer gently for 20 minutes without covering it.

After 20 minutes pour the sauce over the chicken, cover it with tinfoil and bake in the oven for 15 minutes. Then take off the tinfoil and cook for a further 15 to 20 minutes.

When ready to serve sprinkle with the remaining fresh-grated parmesan cheese and sprigs of basil.

PEPPERPOT BEEF

SERVES 6

1 oz / 25g flour

1 tsp sea salt & 1/2 tsp white pepper

1/2 tsp ground ginger

2 lb / 900g braising beef, in bite-sized cubes

sunflower oil

1 small red or yellow pepper, diced or sliced

15 oz / 425g can red kidney beans, drained, optional

FOR THE SAUCE

1 tsp chilli sauce

8 oz / 225g can chopped tomatoes

4 oz / 110g mushrooms, sliced

1 tbsp Worcestershire sauce

2 tbsp soft brown sugar

2 tbsp wine vinegar

2 cloves garlic, crushed

1 bay leaf

chopped parsley, to garnish

METHOD

Preheat the oven to 170° C / 325° F / gas 3. Mix together the flour, seasonings and ginger, and use to coat the beef. Heat the oil in a large pan, shake the excess flour off the beef add to the pan in two batches. Fry each batch quickly until browned, turning once. Drain on kitchen paper if you wish, or else remove the beef from the oil with a slotted spoon, then transfer to a 3-pint oven-proof dish. Combine all the ingredients for the sauce and pour over the meat. Cover, and cook for about 1 1/2 to 2 hours, or until the meat is tender. Add the red pepper and kidney beans 30 minutes before the end of the cooking time. Serve with mashed potato (p. 39), rice or couscous with chopped parsley sprinkled on top.

GARLIC BUTTER

I always keep a roll of garlic butter in the freezer as it is a great stand-by to add to a grilled steak, a plain chicken breast or a piece of fish.

4 oz / 110g butter

1/2 oz / 15g finely chopped parsley

1 or 2 cloves of garlic, depending on how strong a garlic flavour you like, finely chopped

sea salt & white pepper

a squeeze of lemon juice, optional

METHOD
Have the butter at room temperature and place in a small bowl.

Add the finely-chopped parsley and garlic, the seasoning and a squeeze of lemon juice, if using, to the bowl. Mix well together until combined. Turn out onto a piece of parchment paper and roll up. Store in the freezer until ready to use.

•••••••••••••••••••• # CHICKEN KIEV

SERVES 4

This dish was very popular in the sixties and seventies and then seemed to disappear altogether. However, it's very easy to do for a dinner party at home. Your guests will certainly be impressed!

4 (8 oz / 225g each) chicken breasts, skinned & boned

5 oz / 150g garlic butter (see opposite)

3 oz / 75g plain flour

4 oz /110g fresh breadcrumbs

1 large egg, beaten

sunflower oil, for frying

sea salt & white pepper

METHOD

Remove the garlic butter from the fridge and slice 8 circles from the roll. Make a pocket in the side of each chicken breast and put two slices of the garlic butter into the pocket, making sure that it's completely covered by the chicken.

When you have done this with the four chicken breasts, dip each one in seasoned flour, shaking off any excess before dipping into the beaten egg. When well coated with the egg, dip the chicken breasts into the breadcrumbs, making sure that they are well covered on both sides. Place the chicken breasts on a large plate covered with parchment paper or greaseproof paper and then cover with cling film. It's best to refrigerate over night, but if you don't have that much time, refrigerate for at least 4 to 5 hours as they will cook better if they are really cold. If you're doing this dish for a dinner party you could even do up to this stage the day before and leave in the fridge. Pre-heat the oven to 180° C / 350° F / gas 4. When ready to cook, put the sunflower oil into a non-stick frying pan and heat over a moderate heat. Place the chicken breasts in the pan two at a time and brown lightly on both sides. Remove to a baking tray or a dish with shallow sides big enough to take the four chicken breasts. Put into the pre-heated oven and cook for about 20 minutes. Serve with small, new potatoes, a little extra garlic butter on top of each chicken breast and a delicious green salad.

PASTA WITH BACON LARDONS & PEAS

SERVES 4–6

This pasta dish is a great energy-booster; adults and children alike love it and it is really simple to make. Most of the ingredients are things you would have in your cupboard anyway. It is also nutritionally well-balanced.

7 oz / 200g dried fusilli, spaghetti or other pasta shapes

sea salt & pepper

3 tbsp olive oil

I onion, finely chopped

I garlic clove finely chopped

3 1/2 oz / 100g bacon lardons

10 fl. oz / 300ml double cream

3 1/2 oz / 100g frozen peas, already cooked

1-2 tbsp chopped flat leaf-parsley

1-2 tbsp freshly grated parmesan

METHOD

Cook the pasta in a large pan of boiling salted water with a tablespoon of olive oil for 10 minutes, or until *al dente*. Drain the pasta and rinse under cold running water to remove the excess starch. Keep the pasta aside until ready to use.

Heat the remaining oil in a deep sauté pan. Add the onion and garlic and fry, stirring for 2 to 3 minutes, then add the bacon and fry until crisp. Add the cream and let it bubble until reduced by half. Then add the peas, bring the sauce back to a simmer and cook for two minutes. Season with salt and pepper to taste. Add the pasta to the sauce and heat through, stirring, for I to 2 minutes. Scatter with parsley and parmesan and serve in warm pasta bowls with a green salad and extra parmesan.

LOIN OF LAMB WITH FIGS & GINGER

SERVES 4–6

I large loin of lamb, about 2 1/2 lbs/1.1 kg (before boning)

I stick of celery, roughly chopped

I large carrot, sliced

I onion, unpeeled and roughly chopped

I oz / 25g butter

I small leek, trimmed & chopped

5 fresh or dried figs, finely chopped

I inch / 2.5cm length of fresh ginger, peeled & finely chopped

I oz / 25g brazil nuts, finely chopped

1/2 oz / 15g fresh breadcrumbs

I tbsp freshly-chopped parsley

sea salt & freshly ground black pepper, to season

3 fl.oz / 85ml ginger wine

3 fl.oz / 85ml cream

string, to secure the rolled lamb

some fresh figs, to garnish

METHOD

Get the butcher to bone the lamb and to give you the bones — this is very important as you'll need them in the recipe.

Pre-heat the oven to 220° C / 425° F / gas mark 7 and brown the bones for 15 to 20 minutes. When nicely browned, place in a hot saucepan with the celery, carrot, onion, and 1 1/2 pints/850ml of water. Bring to the boil, reduce the heat and simmer for 2 to 3 hours, skimming off fat when necessary. Strain, return to the saucepan and boil to reduce to a 1/4 pint/140ml. Melt the butter in a frying pan and add the leek. Fry for 5 minutes, then stir in the figs, ginger, Brazil nuts, breadcrumbs, parsley and seasoning. Place the lamb, skin side down, on a board. Spread the stuffing down the centre and roll up the meat as tightly as possible securing at 1 inch intervals with string. Place in a roasting tin and cook for 15 minutes at 220° C / 425° F / gas mark 7. Reduce the heat to 190° C / 375° F /gas 5 and cook for a further 30 minutes for rare, or 50 minutes for medium. At the end of cooking time remove the meat to a platter. Drain off all but 1 or 2 tablespoons of the juices. Add the reduced stock, the ginger wine and the cream to the roasting juices in the tin and cook until the mixture coats the back of a wooden spoon. Season to taste, then slice the lamb and serve with a little of the sauce. Garnish each plate with half a fresh fig.

DESSERTS

COCONUT RASPBERRY QUEEN OF PUDDING

SERVES 6-8

In late summer and early autumn you could use fresh, local raspberries for this dessert, which would be delicious.

14 fl. oz / 400ml coconut milk

2 tbsps fresh milk

3 oz / 75g unsalted butter, plus extra for greasing

6 oz / 175g caster sugar

5 oz / 150g white fresh breadcrumbs

5 large eggs, separated

10 oz / 275g frozen raspberries, thawed and drained of juice

4 tbsps good-quality raspberry jam

1 oz / 25g desiccated coconut, plus extra for sprinkling

pouring cream, to serve

METHOD

Preheat the oven to 170° C / 325° F / gas 3. Place the coconut milk, fresh milk, butter and 1 oz / 25g of the sugar in a saucepan and slowly bring to the boil. When it is at the boil, put the breadcrumbs in a mixing bowl and pour the hot liquid over them. Mix well, leave for 10 minutes, and then beat in the egg yolks. Pour the mixture into a medium-sized buttered dish and bake in the oven for 20 minutes, or until the custard is just set. Remove from the oven and turn up the heat to 180° C / 350° F / gas 4. Mix together the raspberries and the jam and carefully spread over the set custard. Whisk the egg whites to soft peaks then whisk in the remaining 150g of caster sugar, one tablespoon at a time. Fold in the desiccated coconut and then spread the meringue mixture over the raspberry mixture and sprinkle little extra coconut on top. Bake in the oven for 15 to 20 minutes until meringue is light brown and firm to the touch.

Serve with pouring cream.

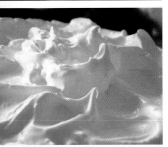

CHOCOLATE FUDGE CAKE

SERVES 12

(see also cover photo)

This cake can be stored in an airtight container for up to two days; do not refrigerate as it will become too dry. Unglazed cake can be frozen for up to two months.

3 oz / 75g unsalted butter

3 oz / 75g dark chocolate, chopped

4 eggs separated

2 tsp vanilla extract

1/2 tsp almond essence

6 oz / 175g caster sugar

2 tbsps rum

2 oz / 50g ground almonds

2 oz / 50g plain flour, sifted

1 oz / 25g cocoa, sifted

2 oz / 50g caster sugar, extra

GLAZE

3 oz / 90g light golden syrup

1 oz / 25g unsalted butter

2 tbsp water

3 oz / 75g dark chocolate, chopped

some fruits – strawberries, raspberries or oranges – to decorate

METHOD

Preheat oven to 180° C / 350° F / gas 4.

Grease a deep 8" / 20cm round cake pan. Line the base with baking parchment or greaseproof paper. Melt the butter and chocolate in a heatproof bowl over hot water and then cool to room temperature. Beat the egg yolks, essences and sugar in a small bowl with an electric mixer until pale and thick. Then transfer the mixture to large bowl, stir in the rum and the chocolate mixture, and then the almonds, sifted flour and cocoa.

Beat the egg whites in a bowl until soft peaks form, gradually add extra sugar and beat until dissolved, then fold carefully into the chocolate mixture. Spread the chocolate fudge into the prepared pan and bake in a moderate oven for about 30 minutes. Stand for 5 minutes before turning out onto a wire rack upside down to cool.

FOR THE GLAZE

Combine the golden syrup, butter and water in a saucepan, stir over the heat until the mixture comes to the boil, then remove from the heat.

Add in the chocolate and stir until smooth. Spoon the warm glaze over the cooled cake and stand at room temperature until set. Decorate with strawberries, raspberries or orange segments.

APPLE & ALMOND PIE

SERVES 8

FOR THE PASTRY

7 oz / 200g plain flour

5 oz / 150g margarine

pinch salt

1 egg

FOR THE FILLING

4 oz / 110g almond paste (you can buy this in the supermarket)

4 oz / 110g butter

2 oz / 50g caster sugar

3-4 firm, sour apples

2 large egg whites

METHOD

Preheat the oven to 220° C / 425° F / gas mark 7.

Place the ingredients for the pastry in a mixer or food processor. If the mixer does not have a top, cover it with a teatowel, so you don't have flour and margarine flying across the kitchen, then blend until the mixture comes together in a soft ball. Next, chill the pastry for a few minutes in the fridge before using. When it's fully chilled, line an ovenproof dish (about 8 1/2" / 22cm diameter) with the pastry and prick it with a fork, trim the excess pastry along the edge and set aside. Grate the almond paste over the pastry case.

Next, cream the butter and sugar together until the mixture is fluffy. Grate the apples and mix them with the creamed butter and sugar. Whisk the egg whites until they are stiff and then carefully fold them into the apple mixture.

Spread the mixture over the almond paste. Cut the excess pastry into strips, and cover the apple mixture with the strips of pastry, brush with a little beaten egg and bake the pie for 35 to 40 minutes.

Allow to stand for a few minutes before slicing. Serve with lightly whipped cream, or ice-cream, or both. I guarantee there won't be any left!

ICKY STICKY TOFFEE PUDDING

SERVES 8–10

6 oz / 175g chopped dates

1 level tsp bread soda, sieved

1/2 pint / 300ml water

2 oz / 50g butter

1/2 tsp vanilla extract

6 oz / 175g self-raising flour

6 oz / 175g caster sugar

2 eggs

FOR THE SAUCE

7 oz / 200g soft, brown sugar

4 1/2 oz / 120g butter

6 tbsps cream

METHOD

Pre-heat your oven to 180° C /350° F / gas 4.

Grease and line a 8" / 20cm square tin. Put the chopped dates into a stainless steel saucepan and cover with the water. Bring up to the boil, add the sieved bread soda and remove the saucepan from the heat; the mixture will bubble up, but that's OK! Put to one side.

Meanwhile cream the butter and sugar until creamy. Add the eggs, one at a time, beating well between each egg. Fold in the flour, the date mixture and the vanilla extract. Pour the batter into the prepared tin and cook in the preheated oven for 40 minutes or until a skewer put into the centre, comes out clean.

Allow to cool in the tin for a while and then turn out onto a large plate with a lip or into a shallow dish. Make the sauce by putting all the ingredients into a saucepan and heating gently until the sugar has dissolved. Bring to the boil and remove immediately from the heat. Pour over the pudding or put into a serving dish or jug and serve immediately with softly whipped cream or vanilla ice-cream.

RHUBARB, APPLE & BLUEBERRY CRUMBLE

SERVES 8

Crumbles are really delicious desserts that most people will love. They are warm and comforting at any time, but especially in autumn or winter. The beauty of this dish is that it's really very simple to prepare and can be made well in advance. You might not often see a crumble at a dinner party because people think it's old fashioned, but secretly everyone would enjoy it – serve with cream or ice-cream.

FOR THE CRUMBLE

5 oz / 150g plain flour

1 oz / 25g rolled oats

4 oz / 110g butter, diced and cold from the fridge

2 oz / 50g caster sugar

2 oz / 50g Demerara sugar

1 tsp of ground cinnamon or mixed spice (optional)

It's best to make the crumble first, so that you'll have it to hand when the stewed fruit is ready. This crumble is so simple to make; rub the butter into the flour until the mixture resembles coarse crumbs, then add the rolled oats, sugars and spices, if using.

FOR THE FRUIT

3/4 lb / 350g brambley cooking apples, sliced

3/4 lb / 350g rhubarb, diced

1-2 containers of blueberries

2 lb / 900g sugar

6 tbsps water

Put about 3 tablespoons of water into a stainless steel saucepan with approximately half the sugar and dissolve. Add the sliced apples and allow to stew gently until half cooked. This will take about 10 to 15 minutes. Turn the mixture out into a serving dish and allow to cool. Cook the diced rhubarb in the same way, add to the apples and continue to cool while making the crumble. When the fruit is cool add in the blueberries and mix gently through the fruit with a fork.

Sprinkle the crumble mixture over the fruit in the pie dish and bake in a moderate oven for 30 to 45 minutes, or until the top is cooked and golden. Serve with whipped cream or vanilla ice-cream.

Once you master this simple dish you can use all sorts of variations, like rhubarb and strawberry, blackberry, apple or pear, or any combination.

All delicious, and good for you!

WINTER

STARTERS

SMOKED SALMON WITH ORANGE DRESSING & AVOCADO PÂTÉ

SERVES 8

3 medium-sized ripe avocados

juice of 1 lime

2 spring onions, very finely chopped

2 oz / 50g cream cheese

a pinch of cayenne pepper

a dash of Tabasco

14 oz / 400g very good smoked salmon

watercress and chives, to garnish

FOR THE DRESSING

6 tbsps extra-virgin olive oil

2 tbsps freshly-squeezed orange juice

2 spring onions, very finely chopped

sea salt & cracked black pepper, to season

METHOD

To make the avocado pâté, cut each avocado in half and remove the stone, cut again into quarters, then peel the skin from each quarter. Put the avocado into a food processor with the lime juice, spring onions, cream cheese and cayenne pepper. Season to taste then whiz until smooth; this should only take a few seconds, don't over-mix as it's nice to have some texture in the pâté. Spoon into a small bowl and cover with cling film. Chill for an hour.

Meanwhile make the dressing. Put the spring onions into a bowl with the orange juice, olive oil and plenty of seasoning and whisk well.

When you are ready to serve, divide the smoked salmon between the plates, then add a spoonful of the avocado pâté. Spoon the orange dressing around the edge of each plate and serve immediately.

BLOODY MARY SOUP

SERVES 2-3

This is really quick, easy and delicious and you can always add a shot of vodka if you wish to liven up the evening!!

3 ripe tomatoes or a 6 oz / 175g tin of chopped tomatoes

18 fl. oz / 510g fresh tomato juice

1 tbsp Worcestershire sauce

1 tbsp balsamic vinegar

juice of 1 lime

4 drops Tabasco sauce

sea salt & freshly-ground black pepper

small wine glass of vodka (optional)

celery salt, crème fraiche, and watercress or chopped parsley, to garnish

METHOD

Place the tomatoes in a bowl, pour boiling water over them and count to 30; after that, pour off the water and slip off the skins. Now chop the tomatoes very finely then add the whole lot to a medium-sized saucepan, or add the chopped tinned tomatoes to the saucepan. Bring the tomatoes up to a gentle simmer and let them cook for about three minutes. Next pour in the tomato juice and the rest of the ingredients and season with salt and pepper. Do a bit of tasting here – it may need a bit more lime juice or a dash more Tabasco. Add a small wine glass of vodka at this stage if you wish and bring everything back up to simmering point. Ladle the soup into warmed soup bowls and quickly swirl a rounded dessertspoonful of crème fraiche into each one.

Add a few sprigs of watercress or chopped parsley and a sprinkling of celery salt and serve with savoury scones or nice, homemade bread.

FRENCH ONION SOUP

SERVES 4

This is a wonderful warming soup — great for shifting colds! Enjoy.

1 lb / 450g onions, sliced

1 oz / 25g butter

1 tsp caster sugar

1 tsp flour

14 fl. oz / 450ml good beef stock

approx 3 tbsps brandy, to taste

sea salt & freshly-ground black pepper

4 slices baguette rubbed with a half clove garlic

2 oz / 50g grated emmenthal or gruyère cheese

METHOD

Melt the butter in a stainless steel pan and add the onions, stirring well into the butter. Add the caster sugar and stir again. Cook uncovered over a medium heat until the onions start to go a nice golden-brown colour, this is what gives the soup its colour. This may take up to 20 minutes and it can't be rushed, otherwise you will have pale, wishy-washy soup! When browned, add the flour and stir well into the onions.

Cook for a minute or two to allow the flour to cook out. Add the stock and bring to the boil slowly, stirring all the time. Simmer for twenty minutes, and then add the salt and pepper, tasting to make sure you're adding the right amount.

In the meantime toast the slices of baguette and, when warm, rub with the half clove of garlic. Set aside. Add the brandy to the soup and allow to simmer for another minute or two to let the brandy heat through.

Heat some nice soup bowls, place a slice of the toasted baguette in the bottom of each dish, put a little grated cheese on top of each toast and ladle the soup on top. Serve immediately with a little parsley sprinkled on top. The cheese will melt into the soup.

CARROT & ORANGE SOUP

SERVES 4-6

I love the vibrant colour of this soup. It's full of goodness and packed with vitamins! Also, it contains no flour and so is a good soup for coeliacs. Don't make this soup in an aluminium saucepan as it will lose its vibrancy and take on a grey colour.

I lb / 450g carrots, chopped

I large onion, chopped

I oz / 25g butter

grated zest and juice of two oranges

I pint / 600ml chicken or vegetable stock

I glass dry sherry

sea salt & freshly-ground black pepper

fresh coriander, parsley or croutons to garnish

METHOD

Place the carrots, onions and butter in the pan, cover with parchment and cook over a low heat for 8 to 10 minutes, until the onion softens. Add the orange zest, juice and stock. Bring to the boil, cover and simmer for 30 minutes. While the soup is cooking, toast some bread for croutons, and cut them into attractive shapes, like stars or hearts. Blend the soup in a liquidizer or with a hand-held blender until smooth. Add the sherry and season to taste. Serve in nice, big bowls garnished with chopped coriander or parsley and one or two of the croutons.

This soup can also be served cold. Chill it very well before garnishing and serving.

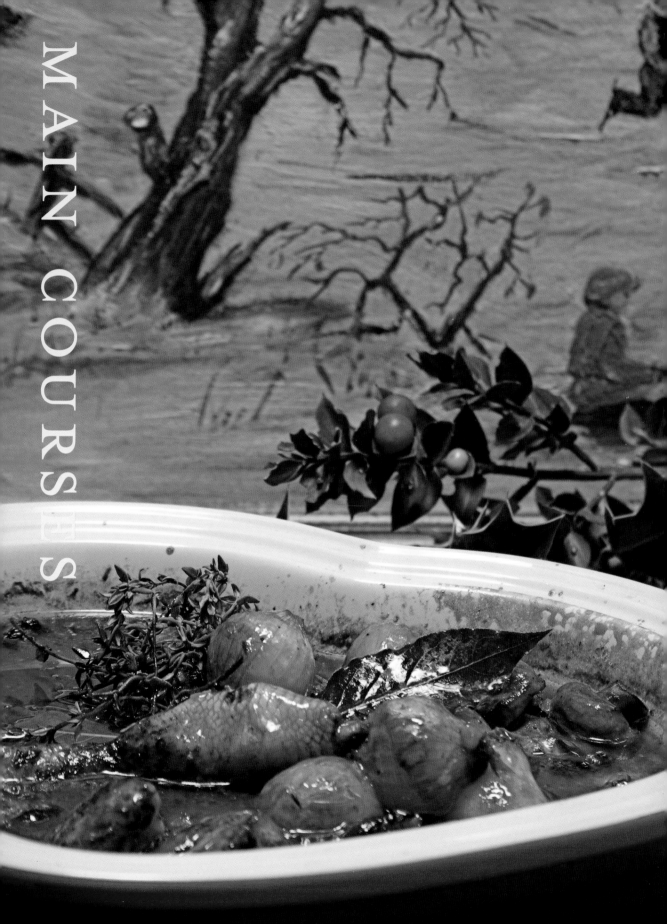

MAIN COURSES

COQ AU VIN

SERVES 6

It's best to start this dish the night before, as marinating overnight really lets the flavours infuse and intensify and gives a better flavour to the finished dish.

I chicken weighing about 2 lb / I kilo, jointed into 12 pieces

16 fl. oz / 500ml red wine

I tbsp olive oil

5 oz / 150g thick-cut bacon cubed

12 small shallots, peeled

7 oz / 200g button mushrooms

I clove garlic peeled, crushed and chopped

3 tbsp flour

I/2 pint / 300 ml chicken stock

2 bay leaves

2 sprigs thyme

sea salt & freshly-ground black pepper

bunch of flat leafed parsley, chopped, to garnish

METHOD

For a really rich flavour, marinade the chicken pieces overnight.

Trim the chicken of excess fat, place in an airtight container with the bay leaves, cover with wine, seal the container and keep in the fridge overnight. The next day pour off the marinade (keep it to cook with) and dry the chicken well with kitchen paper to make frying easier.

Pre-heat the oven to 180° C / 350° F / gas 4. Put the olive oil and bacon in a large ovenproof casserole dish and cook on the hob over a medium heat for 3 minutes. Add the whole shallots and cook for a further 6 minutes until browned then add the mushrooms and the garlic and cook for another 2 minutes, stirring well. Remove the ingredients from the pan and set to one side. Place the chicken in the casserole and cook until golden and sealed all over; do this in batches to get a good even colour. Set the browned chicken to one side. Reduce the heat, add the flour to the pan and allow it to absorb the fat. Don't forget to mix in all the coloured cooking bits on the side of the pan. Slowly stir in the reserved red wine marinade and chicken stock and bring to the boil. Return the chicken, vegetables and bacon to the casserole dish, along with the bay leaves, thyme and seasoning. Cover and cook in the oven for 35 minutes. Just before serving add the chopped parsley. This is delicious served with new potatoes or mash (p. 39); comfort at its best!!

PORK WITH PLUM SAUCE

SERVES 4-5

2 tbsps olive oil

2 pork fillets, trimmed

4 fl. oz / 125 ml dry sherry

12 fl. oz / 375ml vegetable or chicken stock

2 tbsps hoisin sauce

2 tbsps tomato purée

2 tbsps plum jam

1/2 a piece of star anise

14 oz / 400g can of plums, drained, or 3-4 fresh plums, sliced

METHOD

Heat the oil in a flameproof casserole or pan and brown the pork fillets on both sides. Reduce the heat, add the sherry, stock, hoisin sauce, tomato purée, plum jam and star anise to the pan and bring to the boil. Reduce the heat, simmer for 10 to 12 minutes, then add the drained plums or 3 or 4 sliced fresh ones and simmer for a further minute or two. Lift out the pork and slice the fillets into medallions and arrange in a serving dish. Cover and keep hot. Meanwhile, bubble the sauce until reduced by nearly half. Spoon over the pork and serve sprinkled with chopped parsley.

MUSTARD & ROSEMARY CRUSTED RACK OF LAMB

SERVES 4

2 racks of lamb – French trimmed – with 8 cutlets in each

2 tbsps olive oil

2 tsps Dijon mustard

3 garlic cloves crushed

3 tbsp rosemary, finely chopped

3 tbsp parsley, finely chopped, or you could use dried parsley

METHOD

Put the racks in a dish flesh-side up and make slashes into the flesh with a sharp knife to allow the flavours to penetrate.

Mix the olive oil, mustard, garlic, rosemary and parsley together. Season well and rub the mixture onto the flesh to coat the lamb evenly. Cover and marinate in the fridge for at least an hour, or ideally all day.

Heat the oven to 200° C / 400° F /gas 6. Put the lamb in a roasting tin and cook for 15 to 25 minutes, depending on the size of the rack and how pink you like your lamb.

Remove from the oven, cover with foil and allow to rest for 10 minutes before carving into cutlets and serving on warmed plates with some redcurrant, gin and mint sauce.

REDCURRANT, GIN & MINT SAUCE

redcurrant jelly, 1 jar

1 measure of gin

finely-chopped mint, to garnish

METHOD

Melt the jelly with the gin and whisk together until smooth, sprinkle with mint and serve.

NAVARIN OF LAMB

SERVES 6

3 tbsp extra virgin olive oil

3 lb / 1.35kg diced lamb in bite-sized pieces, shoulder will do

18 medium-sized pearl onions (optional)

12 oz / 350g snow peas or mange tout

4 fl. oz / 125ml brandy

2 fl. oz / 55ml sherry vinegar

2 tbsps potato starch or corn flour

2 tbsps redcurrant jelly

2 tbsps tomato purée

16 fl. oz / 500ml beef stock

8 fl. oz / 250ml dry red wine

1 medium yellow onion, sliced

4 large carrots, peeled and cut into 1 inch lengths

5 garlic cloves, peeled and crushed

4 good handfuls of chopped fresh parsley

1 tsp dried rosemary

1 tsp dried thyme

1 tsp sea salt

1 tsp freshly-ground black pepper

1 bay leaf

METHOD

Heat the olive oil in a heavy pan and brown the lamb, a few pieces at a time.
Transfer with a slotted spoon to a deep ovenproof casserole.
Bring 1 pint of salted water to the boil. Cut a shallow 'x' in the root end of each
pearl onion and drop them into the water. Cook until tender, but firm, which

should take about 10 minutes. Drain and transfer to a small bowl and cover with cold water for 10 minutes. Drain, peel and reserve. When all the lamb is browned, drain the oil and return the lamb to the pan. Add brandy to the meat over high heat and allow the brandy to evaporate. Reduce the heat and add the corn flour to the meat, stirring well until slightly browned.

Pre-heat the oven to 180° C / 350° F / gas mark 4.

In a separate saucepan add the vinegar, redcurrant jelly, tomato purée, beef stock and red wine and stir well. Place over high heat and bring to the boil, stirring constantly for about 4 to 5 minutes. Add sliced onion, carrots, garlic, parsley, rosemary, thyme, salt & pepper and bay leaf to the casserole and pour over the sauce, stir well and cover. Bring the kettle to the boil and pour the boiling water over the snow peas, drain and cover with cold water to stop the cooking process. Cook the casserole in the oven for 1 1/2 hours; uncover 15 minutes before the end of cooking time. Toss in the snow peas and the pearl onions and serve garnished with chopped parsley.

PEPPERED SALMON WITH WHISKEY CREAM SAUCE

SERVES 2

2 salmon steaks or fillets, weighing approx 6 oz / 175g each

I tbsp black peppercorns, crushed

I /2 tbsp white peppercorns, crushed

I level tsp Dijon mustard

pinch freshly-ground sea salt

1/2 oz / 15g butter

I tbsp whiskey

5 fl. oz / 150ml cream

I tbsp chopped fresh chives, extra to garnish

METHOD

Mix together the crushed peppercorns, then smear the salmon all over with the mustard and press the peppercorns into the cut sides of the salmon, just enough to give a nice, thin coating. Season with salt.

Heat a frying pan until hot, add the butter and as soon as it starts to foam put in the salmon. Reduce the heat to medium and fry the steaks for about 4 minutes on one side to brown them.

Turn up the heat, and turn the steaks over, then splash in the whiskey.

Boil quickly until the whiskey has almost disappeared then pour in the cream, carefully scraping up any bits that are sticking to the bottom of the pan around the steaks, and bring to a fast bubble.

Boil very gently for I to 2 minutes until the sauce starts to thicken, then taste and season with more black pepper if necessary and some salt.

By this time the salmon should be just cooked, if it is still a bit pink simmer over a low heat for a further minute (to test use the tip of a knife).

Stir in the chopped chives and serve immediately.

COCONUT, BANANA & PASSION FRUIT PAVLOVA

SERVES 6-8

BASIC MERINGUE

6 large free-range egg whites

11 oz / 310g caster sugar

pinch salt

juice of 1/2 lime

1 oz / 25g desiccated coconut

1/2 pint / 300ml cream

tbsp caster sugar

zest of 1 lime

2 bananas, peeled & sliced at an angle

2 passion fruit, halved & insides scooped out

1/4 coconut, fresh shavings, or dried coconut shavings

METHOD

Pre-heat your oven to 150° C / 300° F / gas 2. Line two baking sheets with parchment and mark an 8" / 20cm circle on each. Put egg whites into a clean bowl. Whisk on medium until the whites form stiff peaks. With the mixer still running, gradually add the sugar and the pinch of salt. Turn the mixer up to the highest setting and whisk for seven or eight minutes until the meringue mixture is white and glossy. Dip your finger in the meringue and rub the mixture between your thumb and index finger, it should be perfectly smooth. If it feels grainy, whisk for a little bit longer – although if you whisk it for too long it will collapse.

Gently fold in your lime juice and desiccated coconut. Divide the mixture between the two trays and shape each blob into a circle about 8" / 20cm in diameter. Put the trays into the oven and bake for 45 minutes or until cooked;

when cooked it should have a very slight golden hue, should feel firm to the touch and the parchment should come away easily from the meringue.

Whip the cream with the sugar until stiff and fold in most of lime zest. Spoon the cream on top of one pavlova half and top with the sliced bananas and the passion fruit seeds. Place the other pavlova half on top and press down gently to stick them together. Sprinkle the top of the pavlova with the coconut shavings and the remaining lime zest and serve.

PRALINE ROULADE

SERVES 8–10

5 free range or organic eggs, separated

4 oz / 110g caster sugar

2 oz / 50g ground almonds

1 /2 tsp vanilla extract

FOR THE FILLING

10 fl. oz / 300ml cream

3 oz / 75g whole almonds

11 oz / 310g caster sugar

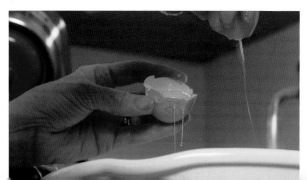

METHOD

Preheat the oven to 180° C / 350° F / gas 4.

Line a shallow swiss-roll tin, 12" x 8" / 32 x 20.5cm, with oiled baking parchment.

Beat the egg yolks and the sugar together in a food mixer until pale yellow in colour, then beat in the ground almonds and vanilla extract. Whip the egg whites until very stiff and fold into the egg-yolk mixture. Pour the roulade mixture into the prepared tin and bake for 20 minutes. Allow to cool for a few minutes, and then cover with a clean, damp tea towel and place in the fridge or set aside in a cool place.

Meanwhile put the almonds and sugar into a small, heavy-based saucepan and place over a gentle heat shaking until the sugar has melted and starts to get runny. When the mixture is a nice caramel colour turn out onto an oiled baking sheet and leave to cool and harden. When it's completely cold put the almond praline into a food processor and whiz until it has the consistency of fine breadcrumbs, don't over-mix or the mixture will become too wet.

Whip the cream stiffly and fold in the praline mixture.

Place a sheet of baking parchment on the work surface and cover with caster sugar, turn out the roulade onto the paper and peel off the baking parchment that the roulade was cooked on. Spread the praline cream all over the roulade and, using the paper underneath, roll up the roulade and put onto a nice, rectangular serving plate. Decorate with sieved icing sugar and some mint.

CHOCOLATE SOUFFLÉ

SERVES 6-8

This soufflé has raw eggs, so don't serve it to the elderly or to very young children. It will keep for up to two days in the fridge.

6 tbsp water

5 oz / 150g chocolate

1/2 oz / 15g gelatine

6 eggs, separated

4 oz / 110g caster sugar

1 tsp vanilla extract

1/2 pint / 300ml cream

2 tbsp brandy

METHOD

Put the chocolate, water and gelatin into a small saucepan and dissolve over a gentle heat, stirring well. Whisk the yolks of the eggs with the sugar until thick and creamy, then half whip the cream and whisk the egg whites until very stiff. Add the vanilla and the brandy to the yolks, and then stir in the dissolved chocolate and gelatine mixture. Fold in first the cream and then the egg whites.

Pour the mixture into a nice bowl, decorate the top with lightly whipped cream and chocolate shavings or some toasted almonds and keep in the fridge until set.

SLEEPY HOLLOW PUDDING

SERVES 6-8

PEARS

11 oz / 310g sugar

1 litre / 1 3/4 pints water

8 large pears, peeled

PUDDING

9 oz / 255g butter, unsalted

7 oz / 200g sugar

3 eggs

12 oz / 350g ground almonds

2 tbsps amaretto liqueur

METHOD

For the pears

Combine the sugar and water in a saucepan large enough to fit the pears. Stir over a low heat to dissolve the sugar then bring to a boil. Add the pears and simmer until they are tender. Remove the pears from the syrup and set aside. Bring the syrup to a boil, keep at the boil until reduced by half and set aside.

For the pudding

Preheat the oven to 180° C / 350° F / gas mark 4. Butter a 9"x12" / 24x30cm rectangular cake tin or ovenproof dish. Cream the butter and sugar until light and fluffy. Add the eggs one at a time, beating well after each addition. Fold in the ground almonds. Add the amaretto combined with 2 tablespoons of the reserved poaching syrup.

Arrange the pears upright in the tin or dish and spoon the filling around the base of the pears. Baste each pear with a little of the reserved syrup. Bake for 45 minutes until the almond batter is puffed up and golden.

Not everybody in the whole world feels like cooking and eating a Christmas dinner of turkey and all the trimmings!!

In this section, you'll find a few ideas for very simple, but delicious lunches and dinners that can be organised and prepared in advance, leaving you free to enjoy the festive season with family and friends.

It's very nice if you can introduce the spirit of Christmas by setting a lovely table decorated with fresh flowers, some candles, Christmas crackers for everyone, good glasses and linen napkins; after all Christmas is a very special occasion and all of this can be done the night before.

'ALL HEARTS COME HOME FOR CHRISTMAS'

CHRISTMAS

WINTER LEAF SALAD WITH ROQUEFORT & ORANGES

SERVES 6

This recipe is very easy, full of vitamin C and suitable for vegetarians. If you don't like Roquefort cheese, you can use Fourme d'Amber or Gorgonzola Dolcelatte.

a good selection of winter salad leaves such as dandelion, lamb's lettuce, watercress, little gem, frissée or shredded chicory

3 oranges (or blood oranges if you can get them)

3 oz / 75g Roquefort or blue cheese of your choice

3 oz / 75g fresh walnut halves

6 tbsps walnut oil

sea salt & freshly-ground pepper

METHOD

Wash the leaves, tear into bite-sized pieces and divide between six serving plates. Using a small, sharp, serrated knife remove the peel and as much of the white pith as you can from the oranges. Do this over a bowl to catch the juices that run out. Run the knife between the membranes to separate the segments into the bowl, then squeeze what's left of the orange to get the rest of the juice out of it. Divide out the orange segments between the plates. Chop the walnuts and scatter them over the leaves, then crumble the cheese onto the plates. Measure three tablespoons of the orange juice into a bowl and add the walnut oil, salt & pepper. Whisk with a fork or small whisk until thickened and drizzle over the salad just before serving.

APPLE, STILTON & WALNUT STRUDEL

SERVES 4–6

1 lb / 450g Granny Smith or Cox's apples

juice of 1 lemon

8 oz / 225g of crumbled stilton

some fresh sprigs of thyme

sea salt & freshly-ground black pepper

a little freshly-grated nutmeg

10 leaves of filo pastry

4 oz / 110g unsalted butter, melted

4 oz / 110g dried breadcrumbs

1 oz / 25g fresh walnuts, finely chopped (optional)

METHOD

Preheat the oven to 180° C / 350° F / gas 4.

Peel, core and dice the apples into small cubes and put into a bowl with the lemon juice, crumbled stilton, thyme, grated nutmeg, walnuts (if using) and seasoning. Mix well. Lay a clean, damp tea towel on a flat surface and place two leaves of filo pastry on top of it. Brush with a little melted butter and sprinkle on a few breadcrumbs. Put another two leaves of pastry on top and repeat the process. Continue to layer until all the pastry is used up. Keep a little of the melted butter and the breadcrumbs to finish. Spread the apple and stilton mixture over two-thirds of the pastry, leaving a strip uncovered. Using the tea towel, roll up the strudel into a large sausage. Transfer to a rectangular baking tray and brush the top with the remaining melted butter and sprinkle over the last of the breadcrumbs. Bake in the preheated oven for 30 to 35 minutes and serve as a starter with a few lightly dressed salad leaves — absolutely delicious!

FILLET OF BEEF STROGANOFF

SERVES 4

2 lb / 900g fillet of beef, trimmed & thinly sliced into strips

2 medium onions, finely sliced

3-4 oz / 75-110g butter

1-2 tbsps paprika pepper

sea salt & freshly-ground pepper

1/2 pint / 300ml good beef stock

tub of sour cream

4 oz / 110g white mushrooms, sliced

8 gherkins, sliced

big bunch of parsley, finely chopped

METHOD

Melt about 1 oz / 25g of the butter and gently fry the onions until soft and slightly coloured. This may take 5 to 10 minutes, but don't hurry it or the onions will burn. When softened, remove from the pan and set aside. Toss the sliced beef in the paprika, salt and pepper and cook it in some butter over a high heat, turning over a few times. You are really only sealing the beef and browning it, so this should only take 2 to 3 minutes. If you overcook it at this stage it will be tough. When the beef is browned, remove to a dish and repeat the procedure with the second half of the beef.

Return the onions to the pan with all the beef and add the beef stock. Allow to bubble up for a minute then add the sour cream. Check the seasoning at this stage. Add the sliced mushrooms and the sliced gherkins. Simmer together for 2 to 3 minutes to heat through, then sprinkle with chopped parsley and serve immediately with rosemary roasties (see p. 37) or basmati rice.

PORK WITH ORANGE & OLIVE TAPENADE

SERVES 2

1 lb 8 oz / 725g pork fillet, trimmed of all fat

1 oz / 25g butter

2 tbsps medium sherry

2 shallots, finely chopped

juice of 1 orange

1/2 pint / 300ml chicken stock

2 tsps black olive tapenade

chopped parsley

sea salt & freshly-ground pepper

METHOD

Put half the butter in a pan and brown the pork fillet all over. When browned, remove from the pan and set aside.

Add the rest of the butter along with the finely-chopped shallots and sweat gently until softened. Add the sherry and allow it to evaporate, then add the orange juice and chicken stock. Bring the mixture to the boil then reduce to a simmer and add in the tapenade.

Check the seasoning at this stage and then pour the sauce over the pork and cook in the pre-heated oven for approximately 15 to 20 minutes. Slice the pork thinly on the diagonal and serve sprinkled with the chopped parsley.

ICED CHRISTMAS BOMBE

SERVES 8-10

1/2 pint / 300ml milk

4 oz / 110g marshmallows

1 tsp of cocoa

1 tsp instant coffee

2 oz / 50g raisins

1 oz / 25g sultanas

1 oz / 25g currants

2 tbsp sweet sherry

2 oz / 50g cherries

2 oz / 50g chopped nuts

1/2 / 300ml pint of thick cream

METHOD

Put the milk, marshmallows, cocoa and coffee into a saucepan. Heat gently until the marshmallows are nearly melted. Allow to cool.

Meanwhile mix the dried fruit with the sherry. Allow to stand for 30 minutes then add to the marshmallow mixture with the diced cherries and nuts. Freeze for a short while until slightly thickened. Fold the whipped cream into this mixture and pack into a chilled pudding bowl.

Freeze until firm. Turn out and decorate with cherries and sprigs of holly.

MINCEMEAT FRANGIPANE TART

SERVES 6–8

FOR THE PASTRY

7 oz / 200g plain flour

5 oz / 150g margarine

pinch salt

l egg

(FOR PASTRY METHOD, SEE 'EASY PEASY PASTRY', P. 41)

10" / 25cm flan dish

15 oz / 425g jar of good quality mincemeat

2 tbsps brandy

2 oz / 50g butter

2 oz / 50g caster sugar

I egg, beaten

I/2 tsp vanilla extract

4 oz / 110g ground almonds

squeeze of lemon juice (optional)

I oz / 25g flaked almonds for topping

METHOD

Empty the mincemeat into a bowl, add 2 tablespoons of brandy and mix together. Make the pastry and line the flan dish. Allow to rest in the fridge while you prepare the filling. Pre-heat the oven to 180° C / 350° F / gas mark 4.

Put the butter and the sugar into the bowl of a food mixer and beat until light and fluffy. Add the beaten egg, slowly incorporating it into the sugar and egg mixture, then add the vanilla extract. Fold in the ground almonds and add a squeeze of lemon juice, if using. Remove the lined flan dish from the fridge and cover the base with the mincemeat mixture. Spoon over the almond frangipane and it spread over the mincemeat with a palette knife or the back of a spoon. Sprinkle the flaked almonds on top of the tart and cook in the pre-heated oven for 25 to 30 minutes or until cooked.

Serve warm or cold with softly-whipped cream.

CATERING SUCCESSFUL PARTIES AND EVENTS

Before I opened The Butler's Pantry shops I spent several years both teaching people to cook in my own home, which I really enjoyed, and catering for large companies who entertained their clients in-house. The caterer's role would be to come in to the office, prepare the meal, lay the table and serve the food. This was a very stressful job as we were under a time limit and had to please very many people every day; they all had different likes and dislikes, so we always had to have a choice of dishes.

I catered for both lunches and dinners and once the day's catering was finished, I left to go and shop for the following day before heading home. It was only when my two small sons were tucked into bed and had a story that I could return to the kitchen and start preparing for lunch the following day. I really enjoyed this job despite all the stress, hard work and heavy lifting one had to do to get the job done; no two days were the same and each day brought a new challenge.

When I decided to start the business in Dublin and opened the first Butler's Pantry shop, I suddenly had a base in town where I could go to work each day, do my catering and prepare for the following day, all from my kitchens behind the shop. Of course we were also cooking meals, soups, breads and desserts for our customers, as well as catering for outside venues. We started doing parties for our customers in their homes; we would cook the food, deliver it and, more often than not, serve the food and clear up afterwards. This side of the business grew quite quickly. We noticed that people were becoming busier and busier in their personal lives and could afford to have caterers in to 'do' the food.

As The Butler's Pantry grew and we opened more shops I had less and less time, and so had to reduce the number of corporate clients we had in favour of the shops. However, today we cater for every occasion imaginable: weddings, christenings, anniversaries, birthdays, surprise parties, Valentine's Day, Mothers' Day, Fathers' Day, St Patrick's Day, May Day, Thanksgiving, Easter, Christmas, Holy Communions, Confirmations and sad occasions too. It's a side of the business that is growing and I have to say that I really enjoy it very much. I love helping people to plan the special events in their lives and The

Butler's Pantry always manages to make them very special indeed.

From start to finish, from the first phone call or inquiry, I love going to meet the clients and working out what it is they are trying to achieve. We have done several weddings over the years, big and small, where a team of us would set up kitchens at the site of the event and serve up to three hundred people. We can arrange everything from the staff, to the bar, marquee, music, flowers, china, glassware, crockery, cutlery and linen, anything the client might need; the reward for us is in seeing how wonderful the setting can be and the pleasure the client feels when it all comes together. Of course the food plays a starring role in the whole event and our executive chef, Niall Hill, and his team are fantastic in providing wonderful, fresh, wholesome and delicious food every time.

During all my years catering various events, I have picked up a great many tips. Even if you are new to giving parties or holding events, with a little forward planning and following a 'do list' anyone can become a successful host or hostess, the trick is not to panic.

The pleasure that comes from a gathering of family or friends, with everyone enjoying your home-prepared food and relaxing together, just cannot be measured. The key is to be prepared and definitely not to take on more than you can handle. Simple food, well prepared and nicely presented, and good company are much, much more enjoyable than a frazzled host trying to provide cordon bleu cookery!

I hope the tips and recipes throughout my book will be a great help and that you get as much fun out of hosting events as I have had throughout the years. Overleaf I have listed my top party tips and I have included a 'perfect party menu' for spring, summer, autumn and winter at the end of this section.

'THE HOSTESS MUST BE LIKE THE DUCK, CALM & UNRUFFLED ON THE SURFACE AND PADDLING LIKE HELL UNDERNEATH!'— *Anonymous*

PERFECT PARTY TIPS!

- Don't ever entertain a larger number than you feel comfortable with.

- Don't prepare a dish that you have never tried before.

- Do let your guests know what kind of evening you are having, formal or casual, so they don't arrive in the wrong clothes and feel uncomfortable!

- If you are having people around for dinner and are under pressure, instead of having a starter at the table, try serving some nibbles with your drinks as a first course. This saves on cutlery, washing up and so on, and you get to be there instead of cooking. Try offering soup in a pretty coffee cup or funny mug, try having one or two dips and serve with chicory leaves, celery or pepper sticks or tortillas to scoop the dips.

- Make or buy a nice quiche and cut it into tiny squares or diamond shapes and serve with tiny napkins

- Serve some really good brown bread spread with a good cream cheese, topped with some smoked salmon, a little sour cream and garnish with some chives

- Little quails' eggs are also a nice starter to pass around (peeled) along with some olives or unsalted cashew nuts.

Moving on to main courses, I always try to have a casserole-type dish in the freezer for when you need to entertain but have no time. Something like chilli con carne or pepperpot beef or navarin of lamb. It can be defrosted overnight and then reheated the evening of the party. You only have to add rice or new potatoes and a great salad.

The other standby I use is to buy some fresh salmon fillets, how many depends on your numbers, and place them in a baking dish with some lemon juice, a chopped clove of garlic, a tablespoon of

'THE GREATEST DISHES ARE VERY SIMPLE DISHES'—
Auguste Escoffiet

olive oil, 6 tomatoes halved and quartered and about 2 oz / 50g butter and some seasoning. Pop the dish into a moderate oven and cook for 15 to 20 minutes. Remove the salmon fillets to a serving dish and squash the juices in the dish with the back of a fork. Add some finely chopped herbs, like chives, parsley or dill, and serve immediately.

As a great standby for dessert I keep some good vanilla ice-cream in the freezer and serve with melted Mars bars.

Other handy dessert standbys are: sliced fresh pineapple drizzled with kirsch; crushed strawberries or raspberries, served with crushed almond macaroons, sprinkled with amaretto and some softly whipped cream, layered in a nice glass.

Alternatively, a whole cheese, like a ripe camembert, or a selection of cheeses served with a baguette or rustic sourdough, some fresh walnuts, grapes or fresh figs on a nice big board makes a lovely easy finish to a meal with friends and you don't have to slave over a hot stove to prepare it especially when time is short.

When it comes to drinks, guests want to eat, but they also want to drink and relax. We can all open a few bottles of wine and you can kick-start your evening or party with a fun cocktail, with or without alcohol, to put people at their ease.

- Try serving sparkling wine or champagne on top of a scoop of sorbet in a nice glass, or make up a big jug of Pimm's or sangria and have it ready to pour.
- You could add a spoonful of framboise, cassis or poire William to a glass of chilled wine / champagne / sparkling wine / prosecco and garnish with fresh raspberries or a slice of peach or pear.
- Try dropping a few green grapes or melon balls into a glass and topping up with extra dry, extra chilled white wine.
- A sprig of mint lightly crushed in the bottom of the glass is pretty and colourful – pour the chilled wine in on top.
- A non-alcoholic offering that is equally pretty is greatly appreciated by those driving or not drinking, so they don't feel left out.
- Always have plenty of still and sparkling water, people are drinking lots more water these days.
- Make sure to have plenty of ice in your freezer. When making ice it's fun to put raspberries or blueberries or chopped mint in the ice cube trays, cover with water and freeze. They look very pretty in drinks.

JUST BEFORE THE PARTY:

- Make sure you are happy and confident about what you are going to serve.
- Prepare the food in plenty of time.
- Arrange flowers if you are having any; a bowl in the hall is always welcoming.
- Chill your drinks and make any cocktails that can be prepared in advance.
- Set the table.
- Put out all your glasses.
- Make sure that you have plenty of ice.
- Have clean bins to take any rubbish.
- Put clean hand towels in the cloakroom and make sure that you have some nice soaps and that the bathroom is shiny clean.
- Candlelight makes everyone and everything look more attractive.
- Make sure to have the candles lighting before your guests arrive as it is more welcoming

Now it's time to party!! Enjoy it.

'SMALL CHEER AND GREAT WELCOME MAKES A MERRY FEAST'—
Shakespeare

FOUR SEASONAL PARTIES

At different times of the year and for a variety of reasons we all have to entertain at home and for some of us the very thought of it is enough to put us off! One of the keys to getting it right, or at least making it easier, is to plan the occasion. I always write a 'to do list' and stick it up in the kitchen where I can see it. Then I can plan the whole event from the shopping to the cooking; if there are some things that can go in the freezer I try and make them a week in advance, if possible. I would even suggest setting the table the night before. The secret is to be prepared and to keep it as simple as possible.

I have recommended a menu for each season, from the recipes in that season's chapter, I hope that they will be helpful and encourage you to have a go.

A SPRING MENU

Smoked Salmon & Trout Timbales (*this can be made the day before*) serve with good brown bread or small rolls

Balsamic & Tomato Roast Chicken (*this can be put together the morning of the party & cooked in the evening*) serve with baby new potatoes and a green salad

Almond Ice Cream (*this can be made a week in advance and frozen*) serve the ice-cream with little langue-de-chat biscuits or homemade shortbread or fresh fruit

A SUMMER MENU

Simple Summer Salad (*you can assemble all the ingredients for the salad in the afternoon, but don't put it together or dress until just before the party*) serve with crusty bread

Blackened Chicken with Sweetcorn Salsa & Roasties (*the chicken can be served hot or cold*)

Italian Fruit Salad (*this can be made on the afternoon of the party*)

AN AUTUMN MENU

Chicken Liver Pâté (*this can be made a week in advance and frozen, or made the day before the party and kept in the fridge*)

Loin of Lamb with Figs & Ginger (*the lamb can be bought two days before. You can make the stuffing and stuff the lamb the day before, leaving you just the lamb to cook and the sauce to make on the day*)

Rhubarb, Apple & Blueberry Crumble (*the fruit can be cooked and assembled the morning of the party, the crumble can be made and set aside*); serve with softly-whipped cream or vanilla ice-cream

A WINTER MENU

Smoked Salmon with Avocado Pâté & Orange Dressing (*make the avocado pâté a few hours before your dinner party and store in a bowl covered with two layers of cling-film, one pressed down on top of the pâté to keep out the air*)

Mustard & Rosemary Crusted Rack of Lamb (*this can be prepared early the morning of the party and left in the fridge to marinate all day in the herb crust. Remove from the fridge about 20 minutes before cooking and place in the pre-heated oven just before you bring your guests to the table for their starter*)

Coconut, Banana & Passion Fruit Pavlova; (*the pavlova can be made 2 or 3 days in advance and kept wrapped in parchment first and then covered in tinfoil in a cool place and then all you have to do is assemble the pavlova 2 or 3 hours before your dinner and keep in the fridge*)

'I ALWAYS WAKE UP AT THE CRACK OF ICE' •
Joe E. Lewis

CONVERSION CHARTS

METRIC / IMPERIAL
7g / 1/4 oz
10g / 1/2 oz
25g / 1 oz
50g / 2 oz
75g / 3 oz
110g / 4 oz
150g / 5 oz
175g / 6 oz
200g / 7 oz
225g / 8 oz
250g / 9 oz
275g / 10 oz
310g / 11 oz
350g / 12 oz
380g / 13 oz
400g / 14 oz
425g / 15 oz
450g / 16 oz (1 lb)
700g / 1 1/2 lb
900g / 2 lb
1 kg / 2 1/2 lb
1.35 kg / 3 lb
2kg / 4 1/2 lb

LIQUIDS: METRIC / IMPERIAL / US CUPS

15ml / 1/2 fl. oz / 1 tbsp

30ml / 1 fl. oz / 2 tbsp

55ml / 2 fl oz / 1/4 cup

75ml / 3 fl oz / 3/8 cup

125ml / 4 fl oz / 1/2 cup

150ml / 5 fl oz / 2/3 cup

175ml / 6 fl oz /3/4 cup

250ml / 8 fl oz / 1 cup

275ml / 10 fl oz / 1 1/4 cup

570ml / 1 pint

1 litre / 1 3/4 pints / 4 cups

Note: a teaspoon is 5ml and a tablespoon 15ml, gently-rounded.

OVEN EQUIVALENT TEMPERATURES USED:

Degrees C / Degrees F /Gas Mark

110 / 225 / Gas 1/4

140 / 275 / Gas 1

150 / 300 / Gas 2

170 / 325 / Gas 3

180 / 350 / Gas 4

190 / 375 / Gas 5

200 / 400 / Gas 6

220 / 425 / Gas 7

230 / 450 / Gas 8

240 / 475 / Gas 9

All temperatures given are for a conventional oven. Fan-assisted ovens often require a lower temperature.

FURTHER READING

For as long as I can remember I have been buying and reading cookery books. They are all like my friends and I get very excited when a new one comes out. While I love them all, there are some authors who have really inspired and encouraged me: Darina Allen of Ballymaloe Cookery School, Patricia Wells, Joanne Harris and Fran Ward, John Burton Race, Rick Stein, Lorna Wing, Jeanette Orrery, Jill Dupleix, Julee Rosso & Sheila Lukins, Martha Stewart, Linda Haynes, Delia Smith and Jamie Oliver, all of whom are passionate about food and who continue to inspire me.

Benjamin Miller

Dariusz Popielawski

Ayman Rizk

Carol Heffernan

Danielle Doyle

Colin

Lenka Pangiová

Julie Blake

Kate McCarthy

King

Janet Miller

Claire Clancy

IVAN KEKOSH

Jake

Frances McElroy

KATHLEEN FITZSIMONS

Kate Dagher

J.A. Bergin

Dominic

Lisa Jacob

Genevieve Lynch

Diane Ryan

Angela Doherty